THE
LIE

HOPE IS FOUND IN ITS DEFEAT

Maurice G. Cabirac

ISBN 978-1-64458-804-8 (paperback)
ISBN 978-1-64458-854-3 (hardcover)
ISBN 978-1-64458-805-5 (digital)

Christian Faith Publishing, Inc.
832 Park Avenue
Meadville, PA 16335
www.christianfaithpublishing.com

The author has taken certain liberties in his quotation of the scriptures for clarity. In some cases he combines wording from multiple translations, in some cases he paraphrases and in some cases his quotes are exact. In some instances scripture references are provided to simply communicate the origin of his thoughts on a matter.

Printed in the United States of America

Quotes from the scriptures which are italicized,
are italicized for emphasis by the author.
If a specific note is not present, this emphasis
is what the italicization is intended.

Contents

Forward

An invitation to innocence! We can all remember a simpler time in our lives, a time before we became acquainted with fear and our consciences were corrupted by feelings of guilt, shame, and inadequacy. Worrying about things was foreign to us and all we knew was a joyful exuberance for life.

In *The Lie*, Maurice captures the essence of what we long to return to. In this simple yet profound book, he pulls back the veil to help us see exactly what it is that has stolen our innocence, and what God has done in Christ to return us to a state of innocence. Like a wise master builder Maurice lays a sure foundation in the early chapters, providing a springboard for the reader to take off from. Each chapter increases in revelation and leaves you wanting more. He builds an excitement and anticipation that does not go unfulfilled.

The Lie will take you on a journey into the depth of God's love and relentless passion for mankind. It puts the heart of God on full display, revealing God for who He really is, and what He has always believed about mankind. This book shows that it was God's good pleasure to take it upon Himself to give mankind His life as a gift, free from our own self-effort. It will help you see the deception that is in the world and enable your heart to be guarded from it.

Having your conscience cleansed from the tree of the knowledge of good and evil, you will feel loved and valued by God, as well as feel love for your fellow man. This book will fill your heart with a joyful exuberance as you walk through this world knowing God is with you now and for all eternity.

Greg Henry
Pastor
Gospel Revolution Church

Chapter 1

Innocence

To find and experience a life founded and rooted in innocence is the highest form of life that can possibly exist. Merriam-Webster's defines innocence this way: "Freedom from guilt or sin through being unacquainted with evil; blamelessness." This is a very beautiful, and a very accurate definition of this word; for it communicates to us that for a person to live a life of innocence, free from sin and its associated guilt, there must be a lack of personal attachment and intimacy with any form of evil in that person's heart. This lack of attachment to evil provides a life platform which removes from the human heart every personal perception of inadequacy. It also removes from that heart all judgment (in the form of condemnation) of one's self and of others. Simply put, completeness is found in innocence, for if I find no evil in myself or in others, any perceived inadequacy and fault would be eliminated.

Even as I write these words, my mind wants to deceive me into believing that such a life in this world is completely unattainable. How can such a life possibly exist? We know that in this world a vast array of evil does exist. This world seems to be more of a place that steals the innocence from the hearts of children, instead of instilling it in them. It is the evil that exists in the world that makes us skeptical and doubtful about the future, certainly not innocent! So how can it be that surrounded by evil, one could possibly find ones self somehow *unacquainted with evil?* It seems such a strange paradox, but as sure as the word *innocence* exists, so does the firm reality of its ability to invade and dwell in the human heart.

As an idea such as this first comes to us, it is understandable that one might question how anyone could possibly find themselves innocent. In a world filled with evil, where the pressures of life have us responding anxiously to the various trials of life, how can we possibly find ourselves 'unattached' to these evil circumstances? I would like you to consider something. In the midst of all the turmoil we may see around us, something remains intact; the person we are on the inside. Though these events trigger emotions in us, apart from those initial reactions, it is as if we are just standing by watching all these events from the outside, making judgments about them. The way your heart interprets these events dramatically effects and determines their effects in our lives. As difficult as this may be to grasp, the human heart, restored to and operating in innocence, has the full capacity to enable us to respond to every situation in a beautiful and appropriate manner.[1]

Though the heart can certainly be affected by external influences, the heart can see these things in dramatically different ways, almost contrary to the way they appear. One

---

[1] Proverbs 4:23.

person experiences a great tragedy and is utterly destroyed by it; another sees the same occurrence and is actually strengthened by it. He or she can see challenge instead of calamity, hope instead of despair, and an opportunity to help in a time of trouble instead of being swallowed by it. Such contradictions can exist because the human heart has the ability to see life based on the platform from which it finds itself operating. When innocence is established in the human heart, it begins to recognize that no external events can affect it. It finds itself free from the fear of things occurring in the world. This is true because the innocence which is found in the human heart has its origins in God. And God desires that innocence be the sole driving force behind all human understanding and activity. And because innocence is not subject to external influences, it has the capacity to dramatically affect our lives, even in the midst of all chaos.

So, what is innocence, this state of heart and mind which finds *no attachment to evil?* Innocence is a rather strange and wonderful state of being in which a pure goodness exists—not a goodness which is contrived or manipulated, but a natural state of being. It does not come through the demands or constraints of law, neither does it emanate from self-effort. In fact, the state of innocence completely excludes such external devices. These devices actually negate innocence. Innocence is a state of being where pure, sincere love and trust are its sole motivators. Yet it never appears that these individuals are *trying to love.* It just seems to be in them to love. A person who lives in innocence and possesses this indwelling love tends to draw others. They ask curiously, "Where in the world does this guy (or gal) come from? It is as if they are driven by the wind."[2] And the love they possess can manifest in vastly different ways.[3]

To be innocent does not mean to be without guilt of wrongdoing, nor is naivety found in that place.[4] Right and wrong have no place whatsoever in innocence, and cannot possibly be found in some equation for the state of innocence to exist. Though from the outside it may *appear* the innocent possess a strong understanding of right and wrong, this would be a deep misperception, for natural innocence is negated if driven by human reasoning and manipulation. The innocent know only good and behave toward evil as if it does not exist; yet somehow knowing fully well that it does. The ability to do this is some form of indwelling art, the painter of which is God.

To be innocent means to walk through life free from any personal predisposition as to what right or wrong is, or better said, not walking through life comparing everything, good or evil.[5] In the midst of this life, we find ourselves completely free from any feelings of guilt. This is the place where true goodness and life finds its home.

In our minds, the possibility of existing in the world in which we live in a state of innocence may seem quite impossible. Without a doubt such persons may seem rare. And I know that in a world where sin and death and law exist, yes and in fact reigns, the idea of living in innocence may seem quite preposterous. But I need to remind you of something. Innocence is the state from which we came,

---

[2] John 3:8.
[3] Luke 7:33–35.
[4] Matthew 12:1–8.
[5] Deuteronomy 1:17.

and if we are wise, it is the state to which we will seek to return. The very intention of God in this world is that we be transformed into a state of innocence and to learn to live our lives from the platform of innocence this very day. For an innocent person can exist and flourish anywhere and in every circumstance. And God's intention toward you is that you so flourish.

As we find our way back to a state of innocence, we begin to see that our lives are no longer dependent on outside sources or others for substantiating our existence. Though compassion toward others is fully evident in the love which the innocent hold toward others, the reactions and disposition of others toward those of an innocent mind will have no detrimental effect on them. True godliness is found in nothing less than pure innocence. In fact, the light of God seen in a human being in this world is contingent on no less. Our being reconciled back to a life founded and rooted in God, is being re-established to His life of innocence and grace. And there is no greater joy in God than to live under very negative, very contrary circumstances, viewing life from this platform of innocence. To live your life in the midst of others enslaved to sin and death, viewing them and dealing with them in innocence, is a life that powerfully affects others. This is exactly how Jesus operated.

Now one might ask or comment, "Wait a minute! Jesus knew sin existed. He knew that we live in a law-driven society and how people have consciences knowing the difference between good and evil (something we will call a *sin-stained conscience* in these writings). He was well aware of all this. If He existed in the face of all of this, how could

He have existed and dealt with these things in innocence? Didn't He deal with people *as* it relates to these things?" To this I must say, living in innocence does not mean living in ignorance. Jesus fully understood the state of man better than anyone, for He was a man, yet possessing both the innocence and insight of God Himself. And yes He did *relate* to them in full knowledge that their innocence had been stolen from them. But in His heart, mind and actions, there was pure innocence, and in innocence, He dealt with every circumstance perfectly. For us to properly deal with others, the mind of the one who is innocence, Jesus, must dwell in us. We will explore these things in detail later.

Now for the theologians among us, one might ask, "Is this type of thought biblical? Are we talking about something that is found in the Bible? Is this some kind of strange new teaching we should run from?" Listen. This is just a book. You can read it and discard it, or you may read it and find it to be deeply rooted in the spirit of what the scriptures teach. In fact, given a chance, I think you will find this book extremely enlightening and beneficial. After reading this, I am certain you will understand the scriptures in a far greater sense than you ever have before. If you love the Bible, you should adore this book. If you have never read the Bible, I believe after reading this you will gain greater insight into the scriptures than many with doctorates in theology. You will find in the words of this book a very different, yet very biblical approach (or perspective), to what is being communicated to us in the Word of God. And frankly, it is this very perspective that makes what will be communicated to you here possibly *more biblical* than anything you may have ever read.

My intent in this endeavor (the writing of this book) is that a heart of innocence might be reestablished in the heart of the reader—not a spirit of naivety, but the heart of a child with the wisdom of God as its guiding force. Consider a child if you will. Early on in his life, you see a very curious thing. The child possesses no fear. If you were capable of speaking and reasoning with that child, you would find that sin, guilt, and shame would be foreign concepts to him. He wouldn't even know what you were speaking of. In fact, I would go so far as to say, children actually do speak. It's just a different language. Their language is that of a life which pictures the very innocence of which I speak. This is why Jesus would compare children to those whom are possessors of the kingdom of God. They simply know that their every need and cry will be met by their mother and father who love them and from whence they came, for trust is at the root of innocence.

Though some may consider this a theological book, it is not my intent to be *theological.* What I mean is, I would rather these writings be considered an exploration or an unveiling of something. An unveiling of some of the most profound truths hidden in the scriptures. These truths are designed to have a powerful impact on the human heart. They do not just communicate the hard cold facts of what the scriptures say. They open our minds to see and understand the very intentions in the heart of God towards us. They reveal the answer to the question in every child's heart and every adult's heart as they consider life and spiritual understanding. They reveal 'why'.

As the scriptures say, *"The testimony of Jesus is the spirit of prophecy."*[6] Knowing the heart and Spirit of Jesus is the ultimate goal of all the scriptures. They are His testimony to you. The ability to understand these things is not something exclusive to me. Every human being is so gifted. God sent Jesus into this world that His Spirit might avail in the hearts of all men, to both the saved and unsaved alike—both saving and bringing truth to the human heart. These truths reveal to us what He feels and what He believes in regard to us.

We have all been taught things about God. Our personal upbringing or religious background is the initial source of our knowledge of such things. Later in life we tend to develop our own understanding based on a compilation of what we have learned in the past, along with additional information provided to us by some other religious perspective which seems right to us. So, our interpretation and understanding of God is simply based on these experiences and how our mind processes and interprets these things. But some form of religion is more often than not a huge influence in what we believe. This is where things begin to get sticky. Religion, in general, is almost always based on some specific traditional mindset or perspective. Yet Jesus, knowing the difference between a spiritual and carnal perspective of life said this, to the religious of His day, "You nullify the word of God by your traditions."[7] A 'traditional belief system', is a very unwise foundational basis for what we believe. Revealed truth, is the only source

---

[6] Revelation 19:10b.
[7] Mark 7:8–13.

of true spiritual understanding; because it takes God to reveal truth.

I once heard someone quote something they had heard, "Knowledge is power." Now although I might not believe this is completely true, I do know this. If I had foreknowledge of some impending disaster and this knowledge resulted in my being saved from that disaster, it certainly would have empowered me in that situation, right? Or if I had knowledge in my career field above that of my peers and this knowledge empowered me to attain promotions and raises, that would certainly be of benefit, would it not? Clearly, having knowledge is, or certainly can be, a very good thing. The highest form of knowledge is the knowledge of God Himself. It is simple and it is true. This knowledge is imparted to human beings by the spirit, for the carnal mind cannot ascertain what is of the Spirit. Yet this knowledge, if grasped, leads to something even more valuable than knowledge itself. It leads to *understanding*. As the scriptures state, 'Knowledge puffs up, but love builds up.'[8] An innocent heart that understands compassionately relates to others in love.

To set the stage for you, it is important for us to understand something. Very good, very intelligent, very capable people are subject to being deceived. If the right information is communicated to anyone in the right way, everyone is subject to deception. If an idea (or so-called truth) is painted as something very good and positive yet the painter has the intent to hurt or defraud us in some way, we are all subject to falling for that deception. Perhaps you can recall

---

[8] 1 Corinthians 8:1 (NIV).

being deceived in this manner yourself at some point. If you have lived long enough and have any experience in life, you know there is a great deal of deception in the world, and from multiple sources. But if you are like me, we all want to believe that we are above falling for such deceptions since doing so seems to convey weakness. Because we feel being deceived exposes weakness in us, we tenaciously hold on to what we believe. We do this to the point that even when truth comes our way, if it sounds different than what we already believe, we push it away even when it is the very truth of God Himself. It is important to understand that very good, very intelligent, very well-intentioned people are all subject to deception. But take heart! Falling, or even living in deception does not speak a negative word about who we are. It just means we are fallible.

Wise people do not take offense when they realize they were wrong about something. A wise person simply recognizes that some error may have existed in his mind, swallows a spoonful of pride, actually learns from it, and then moves on to far greater things, even growing through the experience. Being able to do this is at the root of all true revelation, for no one grows or finds truth who insists he is right about everything.

In the words of this book, I intend to reveal to you a deception. This deception was propagated on the entire human race. It is the deception of deceptions. *I mean, this thing, this deception, looks good, really good.* Yet this is a spiritual deception. Its purpose and intent is so insidious and its effects, so dramatic that to call it a deception is very much an understatement. It is a blatant lie, with deception at its core. The intent of this lie is the destruction of mankind and the very work of God.[9] Coming to grips with exactly what this lie is, and being released from the grip of its power, you will find to be a very valuable thing. In this case, knowledge truly is power!

The human mind is a perplexing thing. Why human beings think the way we think and why we do the things we do have been the subject of a multitude of books from philosophers, theologians, psychologists, and psychiatrists throughout time. I have been around for some time now, sixty-five years to be exact. In that time, I have observed a lot in life. But I believe the most intriguing thing I have observed is the human mind—how it operates, how people reason about things, and how people react toward others. Now obviously I am not the first to have made such observances. All the *experts* I have mentioned throughout the ages have been perplexed about the human mind. Literally millions of books have been written seeking to come to grips with the mind and how it operates. Yet again, the overarching question here is quite simple: Why do people think, feel and do what they do? In answering these questions, it is believed that we might be able to devise some scheme or method to make them work right. I am about to share some things with you. Things so marvelous, so wonderful, you might not even believe it when you hear it.[10] But as you begin to grab hold of these truths, the innocence and love which were a part of your original design, will become reestablished in your heart; with the inevitable byproduct of peace.

---

[9] Hebrews 4:3b.
[10] Habakkuk 1:5.

Chapter 2

The Letter and the Spirit

To set the stage for what I will be sharing with you, it is important to come to grips with a certain reality or truth. Understanding this is the spiritual key to unlocking all the mysteries of truth which lie hidden in the scriptures. It is important to note that this key is not meant for some special or elite group of people. In fact, Jesus, overcome with awe as He began seeing the way His Father chose to reveal Himself to mankind, prayed these words to His Father, "I praise you, Father, Lord of heaven and earth, because you have hidden these things from the wise and learned, and revealed them to *little children*. Yes, Father, for this was your good pleasure."[11] The key is this: God reveals truth to any human being who has ears to hear, *to anyone actually listening*. The only impingement on this capability is our own *predispositions or prejudices* as to what the truth already is in our own minds. If you have had any experience with children, you know two things. They listen and absorb everything coming in to their little minds. Secondly, they are

---

[11] Luke 10:21 NIV.

without judgment, for they have no previous learned predispositions to judge by. Children are thus perfect receptors of information, completely without judgment related to the one speaking to them and completely receptive to what is being communicated. This should be our attitude toward coming to know and understand God, for God reveals truth to those with no predispositions, to those who simply have a desire to know.[12]

Listening to the voice of the one whose intent is to reveal truth to you is indispensable to receiving that truth. Even in everyday life we see this. If someone were trying to communicate to you some pure, wonderful truth, and all around you there were others yelling out all kinds of other conflicting things, hearing might be difficult. It is in learning to focus on those good and pure things above the roar of the crowd that those instructions can be discerned and thus become useful to you. Otherwise, it just seems like mass confusion. Consider turning off all the other *stuff*, all religious presuppositions (things you have learned in the past) and listen to the one who is speaking to you. God desires us to listen and to hear *Him*.[13]

Now one might ask, "How does a person hear from God?" That is a very good question and brings up the main point that needs to be discussed here. God is a very peculiar entity to say the least, at least from our perspective. His means of speaking to us is different than one might expect. As human beings, our way of communicating is by the spoken or written word. God however is spirit, and He communicates in a spiritual fashion. But because God

---

[12] Matthew 7:8.
[13] Luke 9:35.

knows our means of communication, we were given the scriptures, using our own means—written words. Though human communication takes place in this way, this form of communication is carnal (or fleshly) in nature; external words written on paper (and in one case, on stone). In Old Testament times God spoke to the prophets in various ways but always through a mediator, entities called angels.[14] They (the prophets) were given very specific words or instructions to give the people, including the Law of Moses through these entities.[15] But this is the key, the important issue at hand. *Because God is Spirit, there had to be Spirit behind the words given us by these mediators. This Spirit translates to meaning and purpose (intent or motivation). Somehow, behind the written word of scripture there was contained meaning and purpose, but not a meaning and purpose that can be seen by human intellect. This meaning and purpose is seen by the human spirit when activated by something called faith, whereby God speaks to us Spirit to spirit,* revealing meaning.[16] *The human heart finds itself open to receiving what the Spirit of God is trying to communicate when it begins to see something of worth or value is contained therein. This produces a desire in the heart to know. This is where faith is born and truth is revealed. There are very great, very deep truths found in the Spirit of what the scriptures say to us which far exceeds that which is found on the surface.*

So God entered into humanity initially through the prophets' words translated through these mediators (angels) to begin the process of revealing *Himself* to man.

---

[14] Hebrews 1:1–4.
[15] Galatians 3:19b–20.
[16] 2 Corinthians 2:11–14.

Yet because man is carnal (flesh) and not Spirit (though man does have a human spirit) and because his thoughts are carnal (based on the concrete, physical aspects of this life), they could not understand what God was trying to reveal to them, though to a degree some did; those who possessed that *desire to know*. Again, this desire to know became faith within them, causing them to believe what was being communicated. Yet even their knowledge, the knowledge and understanding of the prophets, was not complete. No man prior to the death and resurrection of Jesus Christ fully knew *the truth* of God. For God, the process of revealing Himself to man was still incomplete. Until the resurrection of Jesus and the giving of the Holy Spirit, only the letter of scripture could be understood, though some had a degree of insight. This is specifically why Jesus would say of John the Baptist, "I tell you, among those born of women there is no one greater than John; yet the one who is least in the kingdom of God is greater than he."[17] The child of God today has a capacity within himself, because of the gift of the Spirit, to understand far more than John the Baptist could have possibly known.

So in the fullness of time, God sent his Son into the world. He was born of a virgin, but the true essence of His origin is from everlasting. *For us to truly hear God, we had to be spoken to directly by God, not through a mediator. Nothing and no one else could suffice, and that language and understanding needed to be spiritual. God had to speak directly to and with man.*[18]

---

[17] Luke 7:28
[18] Galatians 3:20

The man Jesus Christ was fully one with God the Father. He was one in mind, one in thought, and one in intent with God; for they shared the very same Spirit. The intensity of God's love for mankind would not allow Him to rest until He found Himself one with man, whereby man might know Him. The desire of His heart was that *we* might share the same Spirit that was in Him with Him, thus enabling us to fully correlate with Him. God's desire to share this eternal life[19] with man was the catalyst for Him, sending His Son to us. Just as the Father and the Son shared the same spirit and intents in life, so was it God's desire that we share in that same life. His purpose was that our heart's intents and spirit might become one with His and that we might be fully united to Him as one. This is perfectly reminiscent of the love of a man for a beautiful woman and the desire in that man's heart to be one with her. God actually gave us marriage so we could see this.[20] To this very purpose was Christ born; that we might be one with Him and that we would be friends and lovers of Him. God's ultimate desire is that He Himself would speak to us and that He would be with us through His Son; our being united with Him as in a marriage, and our emerging forth from that marriage as the very sons and daughters of God Himself.[21] This today, is how God speaks to us through his Son; for we are also the sons and daughters of God.[22] And now, as His very own sons and daughters, the lines of

---

[19] John 17:3.
[20] Ephesians 5:30–32.
[21] John 17:20–23.
[22] Hebrews 1:1–2.

full communication are open to us, as He speaks with us directly; Spirit to Spirit.[23]

And now, because we can hear directly from God, we can begin to see God's purpose in sending Jesus to die for us. Gods desire is that our understanding of 'Christ and Him crucified' be fully manifest to us,[24] that we might see with *spiritual* eyes the heart of God toward us, the intensity of His love toward us. He became like us in *every way*, and in so doing bore our sin in His body.[25] Not only this, but all the sin and death that existed in the world came against Him that day at the cross. The sin I speak of was not the evil actions they hurled toward Him, but the mentality in the hearts of those doing so. The belief in their hearts, based on some form of lie, had them judging even the Son of God unto death! This is clearly seen in their accusations of Him as they saw what was happening to Him. In their wildest imaginations, they could not believe what Jesus had pre-viously said about Himself. This one, dying on this cross, could not possibly be the "Son of God, the one in whom the Father delighted." Certainly God would not let him experience this form of death if He were. Those who cruci-fied Him expressed this to Him plainly as He hung there. They said, "He saved others, but he can't save himself! He's the king of Israel! Let him come down now from the cross, and we will believe in him. He trusts in God. Let God res-cue him now if he wants him, for he said, 'I am the Son of God.'" Their thinking, being carnal and not spiritual, was at the root of their misunderstanding. And so they tempted

---

[23] 1 Corinthians 2:10–12.
[24] 1 Corinthians 2:2.
[25] Romans 8:3.

Him to believe the lie that God had abandoned Him and to enlist His flesh to prove and exalt Himself as the Son of God. But Jesus did not believe that lie, neither would he exalt Himself by the work of His own hands. Instead He trusted God's testimony about Him; "You are My beloved Son in whom I am well pleased." Jesus trusted in His Father's love for Him, as He was foretold by God that He (God) would not abandon Him to the grave, but would raise Him from the dead and seat Him at His right hand.

Somehow, because He chose to trust God and not rely on His own strength to exalt Himself, He died our death to the sin of self-exaltation. What I am saying is, we like sheep have turned to our own way. That *way* is the exalting of ourselves through our own strength, striving to please God and man by our own efforts. But Jesus believed God and not man. He endured in the face of that temptation to the point of death, even death on the cross. He died to the lie that He was not the Son once and for all. It is as if He died as us as well as for us. He did this in order that our hearts might be purged from the fear that God had left us orphans in the world, without God and without hope. If Jesus is an example to us in any way it is in this, "that we might no longer see ourselves as orphans in the world but instead see ourselves as beloved sons and daughters of God in whom He is well pleased." In this very way the words of John the Baptist are fulfilled, "Behold the lamb of God who takes away the sin of the world." For the essence of sin is unbelief in Jesus. It is sin because Jesus death for us speaks a word to us saying that we are His beloved children. Believing that testimony equates to the taking away of all sin.

Jesus became the representative of the entire human race, and as our representative, He has completely removed sins accusation toward himself and us. And now, seated at the Father's right hand, He has shed His Spirit abroad into the world. This Spirit enlivens the hearts of men to believe and to see and to hear. It is the Spirit that gives eternal life to men. It is the Spirit who reveals to us who we were created to be and unites us as one with Him as the sons and daughters of God Himself. This is the message that has been from the beginning and it is the message revealed to us in the *One He loves*. Everyone who believes this message becomes the partaker of everything, the heir of God Himself. And by that Spirit, we are possessors of all the faith, hope, and love that are in Him. This is the fullness and essence of salvation itself. It is not meant for some but for all, simply to be believed upon by faith. Who could refuse such a free, rich, and priceless gift?

As our hearts are persuaded of the grace we behold in the one who loved us and gave Himself for us, we become the possessors of all things in Christ.[26] Though this inheritance which has become ours through the death and resurrection of His Son is spiritual in nature, it is as real as anything that can be seen and it is all encompassing. The human mind, and its means of reasoning, cannot fully grasp the depth of the meaning of all of this. These things are spiritually discerned. Our hearts, minds, and spirits need to be informed of it all by the Spirit that is of God.[27] None of us are fully aware of the fullness of His grace and its resultant

---

[26] 1 Corinthians 3:21–23.
[27] 1 Corinthians 2:12–14.

usefulness to us right now. Yet, growing in grace and truth is not becoming something we are not. It simply means our being informed of who we truly are! Unfortunately, popular teaching in the world today actually fights against God's intentions to reveal to us these life-giving truths which are of such great benefit. What the human mind cannot comprehend is what God, in the person of Jesus, was actually manifested in the world to reveal—the spirit behind the words. He came to provide us the ability to see the heart and motivations of God Himself as He has spoken to us through His Son. Every human mind, every religious mind, initially sees things carnally. We try to "figure things out" by our intellect. But through human intellect no man has known God. We will never 'figure things out.' Even the most learned of theologians, cannot figure it out, though many think they can and have.

So this is where we find ourselves. As the religions of this world have sought to figure it all out, they have come up with all sorts of concepts and ideas. Their theologies and doctrines, more often than not, are based on human intellect and a carnal understanding of scriptures. But this human reasoning can, at best, only come up with rules and regulations and principles to live by (law). This is how all the great religions of the world see the scriptures. They cannot discern the letter (the carnal) from the spirit (the meaning found in the words). Again, these things are spiritually discerned. The crux of the matter is this; in order to judge well and understand spiritual truth you need an open mind, for our thinking tends to be carnal.

We tend to see and interpret things in a very intellectual fashion based on previous knowledge. But what we truly need is not more principles men come up with to live our lives by, but the simple, profound truths of God, imparted to the hearts of men by the Spirit. There is a way you can test me on this. Ask yourself as you read, "Is what I am reading here speaking of Christ? Is there something here that is stirring my heart toward the love of God and not trying to manipulate my behavior and actions?" If the answer to these questions is "Yes, these things do speak of Jesus and what He has done for us. Yes, I am feeling a stirring in my heart toward the love of God. Yes, He is freeing me to see God for who He truly is." If the answers to all these questions is a resounding, "Yes!", then you will know what I am speaking to you is truth.[28]

Listen to these words from the apostle Paul as he, himself, communicates the very thing I am trying to say:

> Such confidence as this is ours through Christ before God. Not that we are competent in ourselves to claim anything for ourselves, but our competence comes from God. He has made us competent as ministers of a new covenant--not of the letter but of the Spirit; for the letter kills, but the Spirit gives life. Now if the ministry that brought death, which was engraved in letters on stone, came with glory, so that the Israelites could not look steadily at the face of Moses because of its glory, fading though it was, will not the ministry

---

[28] 2 Corinthians 18–22.

of the Spirit be even more glorious? If the ministry that condemns men is glorious, how much more glorious is the ministry that brings righteousness! For what was glorious has no glory now in comparison with the surpassing glory. And if what was fading away came with glory, how much greater is the glory of that which lasts! (2 Cor. 3:4–11 NIV)

I would like you to consider something serious. Paul says here that he is the minister of a *new covenant*. And then he compares this new covenant with that of the old. He says the old covenant, that of the law (or the letter), which is carnal and demanded righteous action from men, only brought death. He said *the letter*, or the law, kills. But in contrast, the new covenant, the *covenant of the spirit of grace*, is that which brings life. We will discuss this covenant in detail later. But the important issue here is to consider one way of thinking over the other. The one belief system which seemed so good to us, which was written on stone (the Law of Moses), actually brings death. And another belief system, that of the *gift of the spirit of grace, which is written on men's hearts*, actually brings the *true righteousness of life.*[29] *The spirit of grace lasts forever; and so will all that have come to believe upon it.*

Clearly there is a very dramatic distinction being drawn here. The law versus the spirit. The demand versus the gift. The letter versus the spirit. Life versus death. Yet there is

---

[29] Romans 8:2,

a common thread of truth found in all of the scriptures, both the old and the new testaments, which testifies to the truth of the Grace of God. This *truth* has existed from the beginning and will last for eternity; and it will never fail. Through Jesus, all men have been implored by His love to enter into a new realm of existence wherein the free gift of the spirit of grace reigns in the hearts of men, restoring the soul to innocence as it is motivated by love.

Yet, at some point in time, an enemy entered in... Satan. He entered into the paradise that man was created to dwell in with God, to mar in the minds of men, our image in the face of God. He did this by way of a lie. But God was not fooled! God's purpose in the earth to this day is the restoration of our image, not in His mind but in ours. But for the moment, in this world, that lie reigns. The restoration of the image of man in the face of God is what this entire book is about. As that image is restored and our hearts and minds are restored to innocence, we find great revelation and life. In fact, that revelation is so great that we are told we can now walk in the *newness of life*. In that newness of life, we find all the things we thought would bring us life by our own efforts to be meaningless as compared with the surpassing glory of God's grace, which was given to us freely by God. Let us now look deeper into what the Spirit says about all these things.

Chapter 3

The Lie

"There is a way which seemeth right unto a man, but the end thereof are the ways of death" (Proverbs 14:12 KJV).

In all the scriptures, there is no other single verse which so perfectly captures the state of the mental disposition of all mankind. As we read this verse, it is important to note the pointed singularity found in its wording, "There is *a way* that seems right to a man." These words speak of a particular thing which is believed on by all men; this belief system (or way) leads to very negative circumstances. Because this way is so intrinsic to who we are, I would suggest that it could be called *the way of men*. And this *way* so affects the individual that it becomes death to us. It is equally important to note the plurality found in this verse, "The end thereof is the *ways* of death."

So what is this *way* which seems so right to us? And what are the *ways* being spoken of here which the writer of Proverbs says are the "ways of death"? Let us now read, consider, and understand.

First, I would like you to consider something that may seem off the subject. I would like you to consider the state of affairs that exists in the world today. I know as we initially consider this, our first thoughts might be somewhat fearful, though much of what we see in our personal lives may not be all that bad. You must admit, there is much turmoil in the world. There is terrorism and wars and threats of war. There are huge political and economic issues. There is crime, people doing terrible things to other people for some unknown reason. And there are myriads of other relationship issues: conflicts between nations and even in the lives of individuals.

Why is the world like this? I had often thought as a youth, "Why can't people just get along with one another? Why is there always some kind of battle that exists between everyone?" In innocence back then, I was just a happy person who got along with everyone and thought, "My God! Why can't everyone just love one another?"

Beyond any question, there is clearly something in human beings that affects our relationships with one another in a very negative way, for there is constant conflict. The fact that this "state of affairs" exists is quite apparent, yet the reason it exists has eluded mankind forever. It has eluded us because there is a mentality, or life perspective, in man which seems quite normal to him, and obviously if something seems normal to us, the need to address that perspective would go completely unnoticed. This life perspective is so intrinsic to us that we do not even know that it is exists, but it does! And that perspective results in enmity and distrust between people and even toward God Himself. This thinking is a form of death to us. It is the very opposite of innocence. Whether we personally experience any of the war and terrorism that exists in this world or not, we sometimes find a form of war and terrorism manifesting in our lives as individuals. Human beings struggle deeply in their interpersonal relationships with others. But it does not have to remain this way.

I know at this point you may be asking, "What in the world is this guy talking about?" If all this enmity between people is just the result of who we are as human beings, if we are incapable of even recognizing its root cause, then what purpose is there in even talking about it? Listen, the reason we cannot see what is happening here is that we see life though a filter, that perspective of which I speak. But just because we do not see something does not mean that it does not exist, nor does it mean this condition does not emanate from a root cause. Does that make sense to you? If there was an earthquake some great distance away and that earthquake caused huge waves which inundated cities halfway across the world, just because the folks being flooded did not feel or see an earthquake, they could not say that these waves just happened, for something actually did cause those waves. This is equally true of the enmity that exists between human beings and in their lives with God. There is a cause. But because our thinking is carnal and not spiritual, we cannot see why this enmity exists. There is a *filter* through which we view all of life which will not allow us to see life as it truly is.

There was an event that took place a very long time ago which changed everything, and though this event *has occurred* and though the effects of this event (to a degree) are unseen by men, it has been declared in a loud voice for all men to hear. So what is unseen, I would like to voice to you now. These statements are true whether we see it, whether we have experienced it, or whether we even believe it or not:

"Death has been swallowed up in victory! All the sins of the world, including your personal sins, have been fully forgiven, and God will never hold your sins against you. God has given us eternal life. Everything that God has created, even the future kingdom of God, is ours, and we were created for the very purpose of sharing that kingdom with Him. We have been made coheirs, together with Christ of the Father's entire estate, and we will reign with Him forever. Whatever problems you thought you had are very temporal, for eternity is yours. All sin has been done away with, fully purged from us, cast away "as far as the east is from the west," and we no longer possess it anymore. Christ has made all things right between God and us. God, in Christ has given us His very Spirit that He might show us all things, that He might reveal to us the depths of the wisdom and knowledge of God. In His death, burial, resurrection and ascension to glory, the infinite love of the Father was put on display for all to see. His passion for us all knew no bounds, and all the powers of hell could not prevent Him from coming to us. The perfect state of innocence which we once enjoyed has been restored to you. We have been immersed in his infinite love. The words of the angels have been fully fulfilled which said, 'Glory to God in the highest and on earth peace, good will toward men.' God has spoken a word to us in Jesus which says, 'We please him,' not by our actions, but by seeing ourselves as we were originally created to be, the sons and daughters of God. And get this.

He did not do these things for us because we had repented from our sin, not even some of them. He did not do it because He had to. Neither did He do this because it was *required* of him by God. He did it because he so desired to be with us. His heart could not rest until He was one with us like a husband joined to his beloved bride."

Now, can you imagine that! God established this truth for us on earth and in heaven for our benefit. He did this before we had even asked for it or even believed it was needed. His purpose was to persuade our hearts of His love for us. When this word of truth comes to us and our hearts are persuaded of this truth, faith (or trust) toward God is born. Belief in this unseen reality results in our own personal salvation. This "spiritual earthquake" has its effects upon our hearts as He begins to enable us to see how God actually views us! True *repentance* is not turning from sin with a resolve not to sin again. True repentance is what is known as "repentance unto life."[30] This form of repentance occurs when, as individuals, we come to the realization that God loves us and has proved it by sending His Son to die for us. As this persuasion come to rest in our hearts, we find ourselves understanding that this is the way he has viewed us all along. It is as if the wave from *that earthquake* washes over us, making His faith our faith. Our eyes become open to His glorious love for us. Yet the world in general has only indirectly benefited from these things and in general, it is blinded to these realities. The question is "Why?"

Though the entire world has been gifted with everything we need for life and godliness, as well as the full assur-

---

[30] Acts 11:17–18.

ance of eternal life, there seems to be something in man which prevents him from seeing and truly experiencing this reality. There is a false wisdom found in the world, something in the carnal thinking of men, which drives us to strive to attain the things God desires to freely give us. We believe that either by our own wisdom or through religious effort we can find life. But this way leads to death. The apostle Paul put it this way, "The righteousness which is of faith speaketh on this wise, 'Say not in thine heart, Who shall ascend into heaven? (that is, to bring Christ down *from above*:)' Or, 'Who shall descend into the deep? (that is, to bring up Christ again from the dead.)'"[31] In other words, do not say in your heart, "How can I *attain* salvation and righteousness?" But instead, trust in what God has already spoken to us through His Son. His death, burial and resurrection for us speaks a word to us that He sees us as His very own sons and daughters. There is imputed righteousness in this, to simply be believed upon in order to attain it all. Unfortunately, it is those who believe that godliness (or should I say '*God likeness*') is found through human effort, who will never attain to it. Their thinking is founded in the wisdom of Adam, and it is that same wisdom which has them striving to attain what God has freely revealed to us in Jesus; so they miss the gift in all their efforts.

As a result of this, in this world, instead of seeing life and light and joy and peace, we see something quite different. We see wars and rumors of war, discord among men, dissention between individuals, jealousy, divorce, immorality and every other kind of human confusion abound-

---

[31] Romans 10:6–7 KJV.

ing. And there are all the political factions resulting in never-ending conflict. Even in the spiritual realm we find religions, none of which seem to agree with the other. So men look at all of this, and because their thinking is carnal and not spiritual, they attribute the turmoil to God. We say to ourselves, "In all this discord and confusion; even in the religion of those who profess His name, how can there even be a God? How can truth exist when no one agrees with anything? How can God even exist?"[32]

The world as it appears, contrary to everything Christ has actually done for us, leaves us with huge philosophical and spiritual questions to be answered. First, "Why is all of this like it is?" And secondly, "Is there an answer for us in all this confusion?" Well, get ready, for I am about to share some things with you. These truths will begin to enable you to separate the truth from the lie, instilling in your heart understanding with love and trust as its foundation. In that love and trust, you will find your heart growing in wisdom and in stature, and in favor with God and man. So let us begin looking at what has happened that inhibits man's ability to see life as it truly is; and as it is meant to be.

There is something that drives the human spirit. This driving force is what is believed in the human heart. Though faith is often thought of as something possessed by the religious, this could not be further from the truth. Everyone believes. Even atheists believe. They believe there is no God. Their faith is so strong that they would not say, "I do not *believe* in God." What they would say is "I know there is no God." Can you see how great their faith is? So

---

[32] Psalm 14:1.

great that it has become for them experiential knowledge! But of course, they don't really *know*; they just believe. What faith! And as with everyone, their every action and speech is dictated by that belief. Every human activity is motivated by this inner motivation of faith, for God created us as beings motivated and moved by faith. We believe therefore we both speak and act.[33] This is how every human being was designed to operate. This is also why people tenaciously hold on to what they believe even when they are dead wrong. Though people believe many things, some true, some maybe not so true; the particular thing I am about to share with you is a belief that the entire world holds in common. This belief system is identical for every single human being on the face of the earth. It is the very *way*, discussed earlier in this chapter which seems so right to man. But this belief system, this *way*, is based on a lie. And this lie is meant for death and destruction to humanity. But remember, this is critical: *it appears* right *to us*.

For us to understand what I am about to share, we have to look at an occurrence that took place a very long time ago. Knowing that not everyone I am writing this to may believe this story was an actual event, whether you believe this story is a real event or just an allegory, it matters not. Even if you believe this is an actual event, don't think for a moment that there is no allegory (or a message) behind (or in) that event because there clearly is. What I do ask is that you listen to this story and consider its results in humanity as we see it. This story, whether allegorical or reality, has clearly resulted in extremely dramatic, provable effects.

---

[33] 2 Corinthians 4:13.

If you recall the story of *creation* found in the scriptures, you may remember these events. I think you will find this quite interesting:

> "Now the LORD God had planted a garden in the east, in Eden; and there he put the man he had formed. And the LORD God made all kinds of trees grow out of the ground--trees that were pleasing to the eye and good for food. In the middle of the garden were the tree of life and the tree of the knowledge of good and evil" (Gen 2:8–9 NIV).
>
> "The LORD God took the man and put him in the Garden of Eden to work it and take care of it. And the LORD God commanded the man, 'You are free to eat from any tree in the garden; but you must not eat from the tree of the knowledge of good and evil, for when you eat of it you will surely die'" (Gen 2:15–17 NIV).
>
> "The Man and the wife were both naked, and they felt no shame" (Gen 2:25 NIV).
>
> "Now the serpent was more cunning[34] than any of the wild animals the LORD God had made. He said to the woman, 'Did God really say, "You must not eat from *any* tree in the garden?"'" The woman

---

[34] Alternate wording MGC (based on Strong's Hebrew translations).

said to the serpent, 'We may eat fruit from the trees in the garden, but God did say, "You must not eat fruit from the tree that is in the middle of the garden, and you must not touch it, or you will die."' 'You will not surely die,' the serpent said to the woman. 'For God knows that when you eat of it your eyes will be opened, and you will be like God, *knowing good and evil.*' When the woman saw that the fruit of the tree was good for food and pleasing to the eye, and also desirable for gaining wisdom, she took some and ate it. She also gave some to her husband, who was with her, and he ate it. *Then the eyes of both of them were opened, and they realized they were naked; so they sewed fig leaves together and made coverings for themselves."*

"Then the man and his wife heard the sound of the LORD God as he was walking in the garden in the cool of the day, and they hid from the LORD God among the trees of the garden. But the LORD God called to the man, 'Where are you?' He answered, 'I heard you in the garden, and I was afraid because I was naked; so I hid.' And he said, 'Who told you that you were naked? *Have you eaten from the tree that I commanded you not to eat from?"'* *(Gen 3:1–11 NIV).*

An interesting story, isn't it? Let us break it down so we can understand clearly what happened here. Let us expose the lie of all lies. But first I would like to share a great, but very understandable, misconception. What is almost universally taught, or communicated to us, about this incident is that *paradise* was lost and sin and death came into the world when the man and the woman "disobeyed God." Though this is completely true on the surface, there is far more to this story than first meets the eye. In this story we begin to see the extraordinary importance of understanding the difference between a *carnal* and a *spiritual interpretation* of the scriptures. This is where we begin to see the whole truth. So let us break all of this down so we can begin to see the spirit in this message: *the meaning*.

Adam and Eve's existence in Eden was perfect. What made it perfect was an unfettered, completely open relationship with God and with one another. This state, or condition, provided them with an overwhelming sense of well-being. We see this based on the fact that the man and woman found themselves completely innocent in nature. There was no knowledge of sin in any form, nor was there any distress or fear in them. They were both buck naked, walking around in wide-open spaces and had no thought of nakedness or of sin or of shame whatsoever. This was their state of being. And it was *very* good.[35]

Now remember, there was not one tree in the center of that garden, but two. The tree we are most often taught about, and which our attention is most often drawn to, is the "tree of the knowledge of good and evil." And that

---

[35] Genesis 1:31.

would make sense because Satan wanted sin to be at the forefront of the human mind. His desire was to destroy their sense of well-being and innocence by establishing guilt in their hearts. Yet there was a second tree in the center of that garden, "the tree of life." No one knows how long the man and the woman were there at that point, or if they had been partaking of the tree of life all along. But what we do know is that there was a commandment associated with the tree of the knowledge of good and evil, and there was no commandment related to the tree of life. Eating of the tree of life would have meant continuing life in the state of innocence in which they found themselves; eating of the tree of the knowledge of good and evil meant some form of imminent death.

Now the enemy enters into the picture, Satan. He appears as a creature of the earth and speaks to the woman. He begins to deceive her by causing her to begin using human reasoning rather than the truth of innocence that was in her. He says, "Did God really say, 'You must not eat from *any* tree in the garden?'" Do you see here how deception begins to cause her to question? What God had actually said is that they *were free* to eat from *any* tree. Thus the first *questioning* of God's truthfulness and good intent toward them had occurred even before any act took place. Satan planted this thought in her mind. Then he twisted the truth and turned her attention to the tree that God had warned them about. This is where allegorical *meaning* causes any idea of "simple disobedience" in this scenario to pale in importance to what was actually taking place here.

Satan then proceeded to tell the woman that partaking of the fruit of this tree would cause them to know "good from evil" thus making them "like God." In essences, this is what he was saying, "You think you have everything you need for life and godliness, but in fact *you lack*." So here the man and the woman were standing in the middle of paradise in innocence. In front of them was the *tree of life* and the *tree of the knowledge of good and evil*. A loving warning, yet a command none the less, meant only to protect them, was given by God and an alternate form of godliness offered to them by Satan. Then the woman began to reason within herself that the lie might actually be true—that sustenance (life) and wisdom could be found by partaking of the Tree of the Knowledge of Good and Evil. So she chose *that way*. And she gave some to her husband, and he chose *that way*. In that instant they died. Not a physical death, though that was also an effect. The state of existence which was their life, *innocence*, was replaced with a state of existence founded in believing that through their "knowledge of good and evil," they could attain *God likenesses*. Now remember, God had already created them in the very image and likeness of Himself. But because this way was contrary to their own nature as established by God, the very natural result, (although actually contrary to nature), was that of guilt, and the fear of death was established in their hearts; something that had not existed before. And there is a reason why. Because they had come to believe they needed to "perform righteousness" based on their knowledge of good and evil, any falling short in these efforts inevitably produced in them a feeling of lack and guilt. This feeling of lack penetrated their hearts, telling them they were not as they should be. And this falling short, always seeking to attain something, lies deep in the heart of every man. This belief system and way of thinking became to them a form of spiritual death which would also eventually manifest itself in physical death. All of creation was affected by this event also. Because God could not let man eat (or continue to eat) from the tree of life and thus live in this state forever, He removed them from the presence of the tree of life. Thus they began to grow old and would eventually die physically.

What happened here was not just simple disobedience. It was a choice. The knowledge of good and evil was chosen over eternal life in innocence. And its results are staggering. When the man and the woman made this choice, death to innocence passed to all men and a whole new life perspective was passed on to the world. And so the writings are true that say, "As by one man sin entered the world and death by sin: and so death passed upon all men, *for that all have sinned (or believed that same lie)*[36]."[37] Sin, guilt, and death were not a part of this creation, but when the innocence that was in the hearts of men died, all who came into this world found themselves initially gravitating to that same false belief system. Because the true innocence that was initially found in the earth no longer existed, the option of possessing that innocence no longer existed. *As a result, we all find ourselves believing that by our own knowledge of good and evil we can* attain *a good and fruitful life, godliness so to say and that by the works of our own hands.* We find ourselves no longer seeing God as our source of life, but that we will provide life for ourselves. This is the root of all carnal thinking by which men reason from. It is import-

---

[36] Comment by MGC.
[37] Romans 12:12.

ant to note that every sinful action that exists in the world is driven by this carnal reasoning, this false belief system. In this death to innocence, all sin finds its origin. And all sin came into existence through one man—Adam, for he is the physical father of us all. *But there is another Father who is our true Father, and that Father is the father of our spirits.*[38]

So this is the lie: The enemy of our souls desired our destruction and death. His means was to remove us from a state of pure unadulterated innocence and intimate fellowship with God to a state of being where we would think and reason from the perspective of our own knowledge of good and evil, always believing we lack, always striving to attain.

This form of human reasoning separates man from God (in our minds), for it has the human mind thinking about everything under the sun but God. This is Satan's belief system, a system which brings nothing but death and destruction, and its effects are so tremendous that it governs almost every human thought. Every interpersonal relationship, all of the world's systems, business, governments, and religion, are driven by this very system of thought. That is why none of them really work. Yet we find ourselves placing our hope in the manipulation of systems and relationships, believing that we can somehow fashion for ourselves the circumstances that will lead to a happy and fulfilling life. But life and time has proven this does not work. All our efforts to do so will never bring eternal life. It appeared as if Satan had won.

---

[38] Hebrews 12:9.

But with God, there is great hope. When I speak of hope here, I am not speaking of the passing fancy of the hope found in the world. I speak of a hope that is reality, a hope that tells us what is true and good, something that can be fully trusted. In this hope freedom is found from a life of bondage which leads only to death, where only enmity between people exists. And this hope does not disappoint us. For the hope and light of the glory of God dispels the darkness found in the lie.

Let me summarize, so as to be clear. Adam's choice has resulted in a life perspective or world view, a belief system, so to speak, which drives almost all human activity and thought. This belief system does not come from God but from the enemy, Satan. It has us saying to ourselves and firmly believing that "because I know good from evil, right from wrong, I will make the choices in life to do what is right and not do what is wrong and so become the godly person I need to be. I will *be like God*, and that by the works of my own hands, I will establish for myself a good life, maybe even eternal life." But this is a lie, as we have already proven. And we know from whom that lie originated. This lie brings death and enmity to the lives of people. Yet it seems so right, so natural, to view life this way. My friend, we have a lot to discuss here.

Before we delve into the life-giving truth that sets us free to view life as it was meant to be, I would like to address the potential of skepticism. If what I am sharing with you is unfamiliar to you, which is likely, you may ask the question—"Could all this possibly be true? Could what this guy is communicating to me actually be what is going on in my life and the lives of everyone around me?"—the only way to address this is to look at and consider things the way they are. Just as you cannot see the wind, but you can see the effects of the wind, so it is with this reality. Let us look at the effects that this lie has had upon the world in which we live.

There were staggering effects resulting from Eve's being deceived and Adam's choice. Something happened inside the hearts of the man and the woman. They began to view their lives differently, and they began to perceive God's view and disposition toward them differently. But God's disposition and view of them had not changed, for God is the same, yesterday, today, and forever, and so is His love for the ones He created for fellowship with Him. Yet sadly, Adam and Eve's view of life was passed down to all subsequent generations. Their view of life and God became our view. But back then, when all this occurred, there was a need for God to protect the ones he loved. So God removed them from the presence of the tree of life. He did this to protect them from partaking of the tree of life, thus living in the state in which they then found themselves forever. He also communicated to them that their existence on the earth would be difficult, not because God would make it difficult for them; but their choice simply resulted in difficulty. Then He told them they would strive to extract a living from the soil, and it would produce thorns and thistles. In saying this, He was communicating that their striving to produce life for themselves would not be fruitful. On the contrary, their strivings would result in hurtful things. And so it is today. Again, it is important to understand that this was not a curse God put on the man and the woman, but it was a curse nonetheless. The adverse conditions they would dwell in, their perverted view of God and His disposition toward them, was the result of their decision. God was simply communicating to them this reality. And so we see all the strivings of mankind throughout history.

Afterward, we begin to see some interesting occurrences in man's encounter with the Lord in the garden. It is important to note some things God *did not say* to Adam. He did not say, "I hate you for what you did." Nor did He say, "I can no longer look upon you because you have sinned. Put some clothes on!" No. On the contrary, even though they had entered into a state of being that was contrary to nature and to God, even though the couple saw themselves as naked, endeavoring to clothe themselves, God did not find fault with them.

What God did say is this, "Who told you that you were naked?" God did not see them as naked, but because their conscience had become corrupted, *they saw themselves as naked and at enmity with God.* They had lost their innocence and become possessors of a sin-stained conscience, aware and alive to sin. Yet, what was God's response to all of this? Did He smite them? Did He curse them? Did He speak harshly to them? No! He clothed them with the skins of an innocent animal—an act God used to foretell how one day Christ, the innocent Lamb of God, would clothe all humanity in life and immortality though His own death and resurrection for them.

What really happened there in the garden is actually quite simple. And how mankind and religion (in general) has glossed over the meaning of this event is almost beyond imagining. But they have. In the garden, the man and the woman chose a way, an approach to life or belief system which seemed very right to them as presented to them by the enemy.[39] Once adopted by them, this very belief system became a part of who they were—their thinking and evaluating processes were affected. They fell from a state of being which communicated to them in their hearts, "All is well with the world, with me and with God (as it actually was)," to a state in which their hearts communicated to them, "I am naked before God in my sin." Though this thought was rooted in a lie, this is what they firmly believed. And they began thinking they needed to do something to rectify this condition and feeling of lack. They believed that through their newfound understanding of good and evil, right and wrong, they could reestablish relationship with God and maybe even find *eternal life*. Their hearts cried out, "Something seems amiss here, but I can make it right." Or "I am not as I should be, but I can become what I need to be by working hard toward that end." "I can be happy *if...*" This is a perfect picture of every man's life, all based on a lie. It is as if their new perspective of life caused all creation to look differently than it once did; and they began to grow old and die, as did all of creation.

So let us look at the state of being to which man finds himself enslaved to in detail. You will most certainly recognize it, for it is the thinking (or belief system) found in every human being on earth, including you and I. Just as Adam fell to the lie, we all initially fall to that same deception, the deception the enemy of our souls planted in the world. Though we think we are free, we all find ourselves under its influence. In fact, all of the world systems are involun-

---

[39] Proverbs 14:12.

tarily controlled by the same system of thinking. This is not a conspiracy theory. What I am speaking of is very real and is self-evident. This belief system is so ingrained in the hearts of men we actually believe it is perfectly right and as it should be.

It seems quite natural to observe life and evaluate everything (and everyone) based on our own view of right and wrong, good and evil. It matters not what your standard might be, the life perspective is the same. This is true of every human being on the face of the earth. Thus our life reasoning and the initiator of our actions become this: *I know right from wrong, good from evil. And according to this knowledge and understanding I will establish my life, and that life will be good.* Every human being thinks this exact same way, and it produces resultant actions. It doesn't matter which country you live in, which political system you espouse, or what religion you practice, the thought and this belief system are all the same. I hope you are beginning to see this. But what did God say? "This is the way of death!"

So one might ask, "Where does what we traditionally know of as *sin* come in to play in all of this? I thought sin and death came into the world in the fall." Well, from an outward (or carnal) perspective, it most certainly did. But as with every disease, unless you first determine the true root cause of that disease, you can only treat symptoms. Sin is analogous to a symptom. It is not the disease itself. The disease itself, in this case, is substituting a natural form of righteousness found in the gift of innocence with a form of righteousness founded in your own personal knowledge of right and wrong, the results of which are the continual strivings to attain happiness, with that happiness always seeming to elude you, a chasing of the wind so to speak.[40] This change in the state of human mentality is the root of all sin. But as you will find, there is a cure. And that cure is really good!

---

[40] *The recurring theme of the book of Ecclesiastes, were Solomon continually sought for the meaning of life though a myriad of life activities, as a chasing of the wind.*

Chapter 4

The Lie Manifested in Human Life ("The Ways of Death")

One might ask, "So how does what is traditionally known as sin fit into this scenario? Isn't sin mankind's problem?" Well imagine this. Back in the garden, man found himself in a place and state of being where all was good to the extreme, a state of being in which all our provisions were met, where love and peace reigned. A state in which there was absolutely no knowledge of sin in any form. Although nature itself had not yet been corrupted, it wasn't beautiful trees and perfect weather that made paradise a paradise, though that must have been pretty nice too. No, what made paradise, paradise was the perfect relationship that existed between God and man, and man with man. Enmity, hostility, and disagreement between God and man or between men were completely unheard of. It simply did not exist, neither was it even considered. Another unimaginable thing is that any idea or feeling of guilt in any form did not exist.

Now imagine this. After having experienced such a wondrous existence, imagine being translated to a state of being where we begin to evaluate and judge everything in life. This is exactly what happened to the entire human race through the belief system Adam entered into, the belief system of Satan himself. Human judgment had entered into the world. Not only did we begin to judge one another based on this thinking, we began to accuse God of judging us this way. We believe, within the depths of our souls, that God looks at us and judges us based on behavior related to our knowledge of right and wrong and not on who we are to Him. But instead of this belief system producing life, it produces the fruit of death.

So how does this belief system enter in and corrupt all of life? I would like you to consider this example. Picture the initial beauty we see as two young people first fall in love. A young man meets this beautiful young woman. His eyes light up in delight at the incredible beauty and grace he sees in her. She is everything he had ever dreamed of. Life is good! As this relationship begins, these two young people find their lives revolving around one another. To this man this young lady is the epitome of beauty and grace. On some very special occasion, he stands before God and man in a ceremony and commits to the world, "I will love and be with her forever and in every circumstance." For a time, this is how it is. Then, over time, that commitment begins to reveal itself as powerless. It is almost as if the commitment itself becomes a stumbling block, as things begin to change in their relationship which was initially born in innocence and love.

Unconsciously they had begun believing that it was 'their responsibility' to maintain their relationship with one another, they begin to do just that. Yet as they begin to enlist the power in their flesh to do so, their eyes are distracted from the true source and power that formed and established their relationship to begin with; unfettered love! Leaving their first love, upon which the relationship was actually established, they begin to scrutinize one another, seeing inconsistencies between the love and behavior. They begin to say and do things that violated one another's concept of right and wrong. This scrutinization spoke to each of them and said, "Where did the love go? Maybe I don't really love this person." Then things begin to escalate rapidly as they begin evaluating one another more and more through their competing knowledge of good and evil, somehow never being able to control their judgments of one another. The conversation and relationship, once loving and sweet, based on the love and beauty they saw in one another, becomes combative. Thus sin is born. So, this once beautiful marriage ends in enmity and divorce.

So what was the sin here? Was divorce the sin? Well, if you believe divorce is a sin (and many do), it may appear that way. But no, divorce here is only *the fruit* of what was happening here. It was only a symptom of the way they had begun viewing their lives together. Their knowledge of good and evil had done them in. Judgment of one another had utterly destroyed what should have been a beautiful, lifelong union between two people once deeply in love. This is a perfect example of the death brought about by the way we all think, passed down to us through Adam. There are many more.

One political party knows the truth of what is right and wrong and develops a philosophy based on that perceived truth. Another party develops another philosophy and irreconcilable enmity exists—never-ending arguments leading each other's constituents nowhere. One country's religious or political ideology which is *obviously right* brings it into conflict with its neighbors and war ensues. Every war and every death in every war is over one issue. "I know right from wrong, good from evil" and I will force my way upon you! And religion, what a farce that can be! Here are those claiming to hold the truth (whatever that truth might be) at enmity with those in disagreement with them, sometimes even leading to genocide. Let me say this clearly. If you belong to a religion, Christian or otherwise, that tends to judge and separate you from other human beings, something is amiss. You need to consider the form of teaching you are under. This is the root of all hypocrisy. If your religion causes you to judge people outside of your organization, run! All legalistic, law-driven religion does this very thing. All such religion is based on Satan's belief system, "the knowledge of good and evil', not on Christ!"[41]

I hope you are beginning to see exactly how this false spiritual mentality exists in the world and in the lives of everyone everywhere. It is simply how humans reason. If there is such a thing as an "evil nature" it is found in our being of this mind. Listen to how this confused thinking affected Peter's view of things and how Jesus addressed his thinking.

> From that time on, Jesus began to explain
> to his disciples that he must go to Jerusalem
> and suffer many things at the hands of the

---

[41] Galatians 2:11–19.

elders, chief priests and teachers of the law, and that he must be killed and on the third day be raised to life. Peter took him aside and began to rebuke him. "Never, Lord!" he said. "This shall never happen to you!" Jesus turned and said to Peter, "Get behind me, Satan! You are a stumbling block to me; you do not have in mind the things of God, but the things of men." (Matthew 16:21–23 NIV)

Understand this, Jesus was not calling Peter Satan. He was saying that his mind, not yet being renewed, was seeing things according to the mind of Satan. Peter's knowledge of right and wrong said to him that the Christ would establish righteousness in the world in a physical sense; thus His death would have been a defeat. Christ knew that only through His death could innocence again be reestablished in the hearts of men. So Jesus rebuked Peter's thinking, naming it by its source.

The end effect of the Adamic, or carnal mindset is that all mankind finds itself at enmity with one another and with God—*continually judging everything,* man against man, political party against political party, nation against nation, religion against religion. In religion, in particular, this belief system is prevalent and that is so sad. In religion, where men go to escape the corruption they see in the world, this thinking is more often than not the driving force behind the supposed ministry. They find themselves ministering death cloaked as something good. As we continue to develop our understanding related to all of this, you will begin to see what I mean. But please understand, this is not some indictment of religion or of anything or anyone else. Religion, in and of itself, is neither right or wrong, neither are political parties nor nations, even individuals. The issue at hand is not judging people or institutions, but shedding light on a glorious truth designed to set us free from a belief system that is detrimental to our well-being and brings death rather than life. There is a saying that you may know which comes from the scriptures and is often quoted in the world, "The truth shall make you free." This is exactly what I am speaking of here, for there is only one way to counter a lie and that is with truth.

The lie which I am speaking of here is so intrinsic to human thinking that our every thought and motivation is driven by it. This belief system is the very thing that Jesus died to purge and uproot from our hearts. If you know the scriptures and find yourself coming to grips with what I am sharing here, it will enable you to see how this lie, this belief system of Satan, will ultimately be the downfall of the world. Satan will seem to have won. But the *true victor* has already arisen with healing in his wings for all who are willing to embrace innocence as their way of life. And at the end of time, the very thing that Satan planted in the hearts of men will prove his (Satan's) own downfall also. Just as David slew Goliath with one small smooth stone and severed his head with his own sword, the words written beforehand were proven true, "All the assembly (of Israel) shall know that the LORD saves *not* with sword and spear; for the battle is the LORD'S."[42] David's severing Goliath's

---

[42] 1 Samuel 17:47.

head with Goliath's own *sword* signified that the death and defeat of the Antichrist and his system of belief would come by its own hands and by its own means of warfare when Jesus returns. But for you and I as individuals, that system of death was destroyed by Jesus's death, resurrection, and ascension to glory and by the revelation of truth we find in these events.

More on this as we continue. But as we do, it is important to know something about how God views the human race today. You may be surprised. Most religion portrays God as being at enmity with mankind, distaining us because of our sinful actions. They see Him as demanding righteous action from men and punishing men severely for their sin. But is this really what is in the heart of God toward us? Put your thinking caps on, for we are about to discuss some things that will begin to dispel the lie that is in the earth and in your hearts. These things call for serious thought and consideration.

Chapter 5

Who Is Man?

When I consider your heavens, the work of your fingers, the moon and the stars, which you have set in place, *what is man that you are mindful of him*, the son of man that you care for him? You made him a little lower than the heavenly beings and crowned him with glory and honor. You made him ruler over the works of your hands; you put everything under his feet: all flocks and herds, and the beasts of the field, the birds of the air, and the fish of the sea, all that swim the paths of the seas. (Psalm 8:3–8 NIV)

So what or who is man? I would like to draw your attention to something wonderful, which is written to us in the words of this psalm. David writes, "Who is the Son of Man that you care for him?" This question is very easily answered. In the gospels, Jesus often refers to *Himself* as "the son of man." So as the psalmist asks this question, "What (or who) is the son of man that you care for him," he is speaking of Jesus. These words speak of God's view and opinion of Jesus, having been created lower than the angels (Elohim) and yet crowned with glory and honor. In context, God is speaking of His high view and opinion of Jesus. So much so that He places Him above all of creation itself, even above the angels of heaven. And to this one (Jesus), God committed all of His creation that He might rule (or be) over them in love. But listen to this wonderful thing. God did not say, "What is the son of man that you are mindful of him?" What he said was, "What *is man* that you are mindful of him?" Then afterward, "The son of man, that you care for him?" So in God's own marvelously well-worded speech, God speaks of Jesus and man (that is the human race) *in the very same breath*, as if we were one with him!

This may blow your mind, but God does not view us as despicable sinners He hates until we somehow get it right. One might ask, "How exactly does he view us?" He views us with all the value in which He sees His one and only Son, and He sent His Son to reveal this to us! In His mind, it has always been this way, for His work was finished from the creation of the world.[43] Man's problem is not how God views us, but the flawed way we perceive the way He views us. We see ourselves in relation to him through a sin-stained consciousness. We believe he views us, through our own faulty belief system, based on our external actions and the knowledge of *good and evil*. Due to our faulty belief sys-

---

[43] Hebrews 4:3.

tem, we think He sees us in sin. It is as if when we look at God, a veil exists in our minds. Everything we see coming to us from Him seems to be based on our perception of ourselves and our behavior. We believe we can approach God only if our behavior is right (which we determine by our own knowledge of good and evil), thus we actually alienate *ourselves* from God, even though He has fully taken away our sins at the cross. If we understood that there is no sin in Him, we would know that there is no sin in us, for He has made us one with Him. Listen to these words from the Song of Solomon. "You are altogether beautiful, my darling; there is no flaw in you."[44] Understand that these are not just some flowery words meant to make us feel good as we read them. They are powerful intrinsic truths written to help us see God's view of Jesus and His view and opinion of us as well. But our consciences will not let us see this. They are stained with a consciousness of sin and only in Jesus is that veil taken away. God sees us through Jesus, even as Jesus.[45]

I know some, in particular those with deep religious backgrounds, may question what I am sharing. Someone might ask, "Is not man separated from God because of his sin? How can God look upon a human being with such a view if sin exists in his heart? Does not man, prior to salvation, have a sinful nature needing to be rectified by salvation? What about people whose actions are utterly evil... I mean really bad people? Does God see them this way?" But in these very questions we testify against ourselves, using

---

[44] Song of Songs.
[45] 2 Corinthians 3:15–18.

the Adamic mindset to judge others. *We are actually imputing to men the very sin Jesus died to take away from them.* Can you see that? All this is due to our own lack of understanding, seeing things through this sin-stained conscience. We go way too far in our judgments, our every thought judging things, both God and man, through our knowledge of good and evil *and not through what was revealed in Jesus.* This is where coming to understand the spirit of scripture begins to require a huge paradigm shift in the thinking of the human heart. In our own understanding, we cannot imagine how God could possibly view mankind in this way. He sees us as holy, righteous, and blameless before Him. To begin to see this clearly, we need to have a clear understanding of the gospel itself and how the gospel works in the human heart.

The Gospel communicates something to us that is totally contrary to the way we naturally think; whether you are an individual who has a religious background, or someone who simply believes you are a good person. Each of us has some standard by which we judge ourselves and others. But whether it be the law of Moses or your own personal standards, everyone has some standard. The problem with living according to external standards is that we never find ourselves truly meeting even the standards we create for ourselves. And I guarantee you this. The people around you will most certainly miss that mark of righteousness *you* set for them! These failures, not just ours, but the failures of others we are judging by these standards, brings nothing but guilt and a feeling of lack deep within our hearts. And these standards and laws can never produce the fruit God desires to bestow upon us apart from our works.

The Gospel is not based on external standards. It tells us that we are loved and accepted by God completely apart from our works. It speaks to us of our innocence before God. The unique part of all this is simply this. Just as we once judged everyone (including ourselves), by our own weak standards of right and wrong, resulting in our being at enmity with others, producing in us feelings of guilt and lack. So now we find ourselves under the judgement of God. He has judged us acceptable and declared us righteous at the cross in love. Here we find empowerment to love and accept others, our guilt having been swallowed up in victory. We have been made partakers of eternal life, the eternal life that is in Him. We now find ourselves complete and lacking nothing. Understanding these things enables the fruit of God's Spirit; love, joy, peace, patience, gentleness and kindness to spring forth in us

The law speaks a word to us that tells us we are unholy, unworthy. It brings guilt and condemnation to our hearts and the feeling of constant striving. But Christ speaks a word to us that says we are holy and very worthy! Not necessarily according to our actions, but according to the view and opinion of us which He clearly communicated to us at the cross. The apostle Paul put it this way in the book of Galatians, as he speaks to us in a very facetious way.

"Is the law, therefore, opposed to the promises of God? Absolutely not! For if a law had been given that could impart life, then righteousness would certainly have come by the law" (Gal. 3:21).

Paul knew that *true life* is not found in laws or principles or by the work of human hands. He knew that no one could somehow *work up* life. Life is found in God, and life is what men need. John put it this way, "In Him was life, and that life was the light of men." It is the Spirit of God which imparts life to man. Though the Spirit of God is a very real entity, a part of the makeup of God Himself, it is important to note that in that Spirit is also contained an idea or a truth. In that Spirit, there is a word spoken to us which says something about us in relation to God. It says, "We are the very Children of God Himself."[46] For in the Spirit of God we find the mind of God toward us. As an example of what I am saying, consider that I have a spirit inside of me that just loves people. Now this is *my* spirit and the way *I* view people. But If I could somehow impart that spirit *to you*, then you too *would be just like me, fully loving people.* Though this may be a hypothetical example, we remove the hypothetical when we see that God had that very spirit within Him toward us. And He imparts that very Spirit to us when we see and experience the heart of God displayed toward us in His death and resurrection for us.

Jesus's death, burial, resurrection, and ascension to glory *speak a spiritual word* to us and about us. It tells us that God fully loves and accepts us totally apart from our works and regardless of sin. This specifically is why Jesus is referred to as "the Word of God." As we come to see and believe (or internalize) this truth, the same Spirit that was in Him comes to us. God's Spirit is thereby conjoined with ours and His eternal life is established in our hearts. Our lives are completely fulfilled by this wonderful *life-giving* reality as forgiveness and eternal life becomes firmly established in our hearts. The heart and mind of a human being

---

[46] Romans 8:16.

can find itself in no better place than that of resting in the security of knowing that we are fully loved by God, knowing that this love seeks only good for the ones He loves. The apostle Paul expressed it this way, "The life I live in this body, I live by *the faith of the Son of God* who loved me and gave Himself for me."[47] Our life is born not of *our faith*, but of *His faith (or expression of love)* toward us.

Remember we spoke earlier of the true nature of sin. When I speak of sin here, I mean the sinful actions of men. From here on out, I will refer to these actions as the "fruit of the flesh," for that is exactly what sin is. All sin stems from a belief system innate to man saying, "By my efforts and good deeds, I will establish myself in life." The whole world believes this way. The thought is this, "*I know right from wrong, good from evil, and I will provide for myself a good life through the works of my own hands.*" This sin can be seen in someone's religious attempts to obey all the laws of his religion, which will only reap the fruit of the flesh (as was evidenced in the lives of the Pharisees) or some young man believing a relationship with some other man's wife will be good for him, fulfilling his dreams. Believe it or not, these two examples are no different. Both individuals believe they know right from wrong, good from evil, and both are setting forth to provide life for themselves by the works of their own hands. But this belief system can only produce the fruit of the flesh (sin) and ultimately death. One man's efforts, such as the Pharisees', resulted in the crucifixion of the Son of God; the other one resulted in adultery. The Spirit of Christ is utterly opposed to the

---

[47] Galatians 2:20.

religious hypocrisy found in legalistic religion. There is no difference between a religionist and an adulterer. But honestly, considering the fruit which was actually manifesting in these examples, I think I would rather be found an adulterer, than among those who crucified the Lord of Glory.

But in all this confused thinking, God sees something in man that is well worth saving. He sees a beauty in us that He deeply desires to be with. No one has ever looked at his own newborn child and said, "What a despicable thing! Don't you know that this child has a sinful nature, that this child was born in sin?" No! We look at that child and say, "What innocence! What beauty! This child is bone of my bone, flesh of my flesh! This is MY CHILD! I see nothing but beauty and perfection in her (or him)!" This is the same heart God has toward us, for we proceeded forth and came from Him. He is the Rock from which we were hewn.[48] And this was no less the motivation in His heart when He died for us. He did not just think it was a neat thing to do.

God has great passion in his heart toward us, for He beheld in us great value and worth. He saw within us beauty, when by all outward appearances we saw Him as an enemy. So this was what was (and is) in His heart toward us, *I want to make those I love more than my own life the very beauty I behold in them.* Now I would like to recount for you exactly how His heart accomplished this.

Something earth-shattering happened during that period when Christ died and was raised from the dead. Throughout the events of those days, the texts of the scriptures paint for us word pictures. These word pictures are

---

[48] Isaiah 51:1.

meant to reveal to us the *meaning* of the events themselves. I would like you to remember with me. Remember the cross Jesus carried? This cross represented the work of man's hands, his labor. It was analogous to our sin of striving for life and righteousness through our own efforts, but which yields only death. That cross became death to Him also, just as it was death to us. And that cross was placed on Jesus's back as He bore that burden with us and for us all. It is important to note here how He shared that burden with *a man* called Simeon (signifying that He was sharing the burden and weight of our own efforts with us, even as us). The cross tells us he was taking upon himself all mans efforts to find righteousness through the flesh upon himself (the sin of mankind). And to that cross of self effort He was nailed and died, signifying mans death to that system of righteousness. He became a curse as He became attached to the very lie which held us in the bonds of the fear of death, thus lending meaning to the scriptures which say "Cursed is anyone who is nailed to a tree." And as He hung there, He uttered these words, "Father, forgive them, for they know not what they do."[49] From the cross, He divorced us from our sin as He died to that *sin system* once and for all. This speaks a powerful word to us, telling us we are no longer bound to a system of human effort anymore. Now we can live a life driven by the desires in His heart which have become our passion.

The sin of crucifying a completely innocent man, a man who just happened to be the one sent by God to bless the people of the world, is the sin of all sins. So what does

---

[49] Luke 23:34 KJV.

Jesus do in response to the sin of sins? What vengeance does He take upon them? He does but one thing. He recognizes the blindness and helpless state of those whom He loved, and He forgives them. Contrary to taking vengeance, contrary to every human way of thinking, He thought not of Himself, but, He thought of us. He could have said, 'I know who I am, and I'll prove it.' But think! That would be living by the same self-exalting system that we had adopted. But Jesus would not yield to that voice of death. Instead He died to that belief system once for all. In doing so He revealed a new belief system whereby we might believe in and live. God's testimony, *that He was His beloved Son in whom He was well pleased,* can now become our own! His faith can be our faith and by that faith we are saved.

So listen. This is critical. Jesus died just as we die. He died at the hands of the very system of thinking (or belief) that caused our death, and He died as a victim to that system of thinking just as we die a victim to it. To be more explicit, *He died as us, as if He were us.* Jesus has now become the true representative of the human race before God, just as Adam once was. Now, in lieu of seeing ourselves fearful of God seeing ourselves in sin, we find ourselves being drawn to God because we know He loves us and sees us as if we were His own sons and daughters.

At the cross, we also died. Because Jesus is the true representative of man before the face of God, everything that is true of Jesus is now true of us. Thus, we can see ourselves dead to any form of work-based system of righteousness for life, no longer trusting our knowledge of good and evil to work salvation for ourselves but trusting God to raise our physical bodies from the dead just as He did Jesus's. In Him, we die to self-effort and come alive to a testimony. Just as God, at Jesus's baptism, looked at Jesus and said, "This is my beloved Son in whom I am well pleased," that testimony is fully true of us also! God took a man, Jesus, and put our sin on Him. This caused Jesus to appear exactly like us. And in that very state (full of our sin), Jesus trusted in the testimony of God toward Him. Jesus knew and trusted God, that even in the midst of possessing the sin of all mankind, God would raise Him from the dead. This trust resulted in Jesus's own salvation from death, and as we believe this, it results in our own salvation from that death as well.[50] The testimony of God toward His Son, dead in our sins, becomes the testimony of God toward us as we find ourselves dead in our sins. "You are now His beloved son or daughter, in whom He is well pleased!" Listen to these beautiful words from scripture that say the same thing:

> We accept man's testimony, but God's testimony is greater because it is the testimony *of God*, which He has given about His Son. Anyone who believes in the Son of God has this testimony in his heart. Anyone who does not believe God has made Him out to be a liar, because he has not believed the testimony God has given about His Son. And this is the testimony: God has given us eternal life, and this life is in His Son. He who has the Son has

---

[50] Hebrews 2:10.

life; he who does not have the Son of God does not have life. I write these things to you who believe in the name of the Son of God so that you may know that you have eternal life. (1 John 5:9–13 NIV)

So who or what is man? All mankind, from God's perspective, are fully loved and accepted by God. This was clearly communicated to us in Jesus's heart toward us at the cross. Just as Jesus believed God's testimony toward Him as He hung on the cross *dead in our sins*, so we can now believe that this is also God's testimony toward us. We too are His "beloved sons and daughters in whom He is well pleased." This is the point where Jesus's faith becomes our own and where we find what God's heart toward us really is. And as we believe this glorious truth, we find ourselves no longer dead in our sins but fully alive to God in Christ. This is specifically why Jesus would tell the religious leaders of his day, "If you believe not that I am He, you will die in your sins."[51] But oh, how good it is to simply believe and to find yourself fully clothed in His righteousness; to have believed in His good view and opinion of you! Yes, this is who man is! And this is why it is by faith that this righteousness is entered into!

---

[51] John 8:24.

Chapter 6

What Is Religion?

One of the greatest blessings of God in Christ is that as we begin seeing His grace toward us. He *begins* to remove all judgment from our heart. When I say there is no judgment, I mean judgment by comparison. I know longer look at what others believe versus what I believe and judge or belittle their thinking, nor do I look at and weigh another man's value above or below that of my own based on their behavior. In innocence and truth, I may be in a conversation with someone and think to myself, "My God, how can that person believe like that!" Yet in a heart of love and innocence, as completely screwed up as their thinking might truly be, I find myself existing in and around such folks, never judging.[52] In truth, I can understand that differences exist and just love these folks. Yet I can share what I have come to understand with others in love, trusting God to bring about understanding in their hearts and mine also. I never have to look down on anyone, neither do I have to *force* what I believe on others. Innocence toward

---

[52] John 8:15.

others says, "It is not mine to convince anyone, my Father in heaven is quite capable of that."

As we begin to discuss the idea of religion, it is important to note one rather astounding and immutable fact. Christ did not come to this earth to establish a religion at all! Nowhere in the scriptures does it say, 'This is the religion I have chosen'. Neither is the body of Christ characterized by a compilation of multiple groups of disconnected groups of churches. In fact, the scriptures do not even say that 'Christianity' is now the religion. Though there are many who claim to be 'the religion', using longevity or scripture taken out of context to substantiate these claims, no such religion is so named in the scriptures because no such religion exists!

No, Christ did not come to establish religion. He came to establish Himself in the hearts of men. This one truth should utterly revolutionize your perspective of God and His intentions toward you. You, as an individual, are more important to God than all the religions of the world! God has the full capacity to view you in this way. As a part of His physical body on earth, His mind (or Spirit) within you has the full capability of causing you to function perfectly as a part of that body. His Spirit within you is what causes Him to be the controlling influence in your life (your head). Yet, even though there is a very real 'individual' aspect of the body of Christ, there is also groups of people who meet together 'as the church'. This too is a good thing. These bodies of believers are also meant to function as a body, as the individuals within these groups build one another up in the faith, which is Jesus.

So let us look at religion. The primary focus of religion is behavior. This may not be overtly communicated. Usually religion communicates to us that their focus is God and a relationship with God. But it is almost exclusively communicated to us in religion that this relationship with God is dependent on good behavior and always contains some form of means to atoning for poor behavior. Practically all human religion is based on these premises. But consider this. If my behavior is the key to providing me relationship and fellowship with God, exactly how good does one have to be? The intricacies of such a relationship would be phenomenal and the level of righteousness indeterminable. The individuals believing this way would be constantly trying to figure out their status in God's eyes and never quite find that out. Sound familiar at all? It should, for it is the source of spiritual frustration in the hearts of most people found in religious culture today who find themselves forever seeking but never really finding the truth.[53]

If we use the idea of keeping the law of Moses, the Ten Commandments, as a gauge to determine our standing before God or our establishing relationship with God, would this truly be an effective means? Examining ourselves in relation to the law in such a fashion only speaks one word to you, and about you. It Says, "You fall short! For *no one* truly obeys these commandments." And if someone says, "When you transgress, just confess and He will forgive you." Well, to this I must say, "Exactly what degree of sin requires such confession for fellowship to be restored?" Even if I thought I knew that answer, I could be wrong.

---

[53] 2 Timothy 3:7.

Such a relationship with God would be very tenuous and spasmodic to say the least. And I can guarantee you this: it will never provide you with the *streams of living water* promised to His children through a life founded in innocence! Relationship based on behavior inevitably results in self-judgment and guilt as well as judgment of others. As we consider these things, do you not think it may be time to begin rethinking our spiritual perspective of life and religion?

So now let us consider behavior since it is so intrinsically tied to religion. There is no question that there is some tie between real truth and overt human action. Yet these things interface in far different ways than religion has traditionally communicated to us. Good and evil do exist. Murder, adultery, and rape and all the other things the law speaks against are certainly evil. Not lying to someone, not stealing from them, loving your neighbor, and loving God are certainly good. Though we innately know good from evil and though the law spells it all out for us plainly, none of us seem to have the ability to fulfill that law, or even come close to fulfilling it. The only thing the law does is leaves us frustrated, *believing* there is "no answer for our situation." This is specifically why the scripture says, "The law is *not* of faith".[54] In fact that very scripture goes on to say, "The man that doeth them shall live by them."[55] In other words, the man who lives by the law finds himself a transgressor of the law. Human beings living in the mindset of Adam, believing they can clothe themselves by their

---

[54] Galatians 3:12.
[55] Romans 10:5.

outward actions, find themselves trapped in a cycle of sin and death that will never end. It is only in finding and being restored to innocence (called justification) that we can be set free from this endless cycle of sin and death. So let us be blatantly honest here. It is time to face the truth! Religion (in general) does not want you to believe that you are fully justified, for in the day you are, you will no longer need them.

In Christ, God has completely destroyed the lie found in the Adamic belief system. He did this by revealing to us the truth of how He truly views us as "His beloved sons and daughters in whom he is well pleased." He did not do this without reason. His purpose in all of this was that we might see that this is how He has viewed us, even from the beginning[56], that we might view ourselves that very way, as innocent before Him in love. Believing God's testimony toward us in Christ, we no longer need to operate from the mental or spiritual platform of good and evil. We can now view everything in life from a platform of innocence because we are innocent! As a result we can perceive life clearly, and we begin to see people differently also. For now we can see people in love, seeing past their evil behavior (though not condoning that behavior) and deal with the individual as the person truly is, knowing that they are loved by God and seen as beautiful (the person, not the behavior). But there is a key to this ability. We need to see *ourselves* as divorced from all sin or justified before God, in order that we can see others in this fashion also. Just as Jesus divorced or completely separated you from your sin, you can now see and

---

[56] John 15:26–27.

deal with others as divorced from their sin (or apart from their sin). This is where love toward others is born in our hearts. Otherwise we only find ourselves judging and condemning others. This is indicative of the religious hypocrisy we see in religion; men and women judging others and even God according to the flesh, looking at the external actions of God and man and judging them based on what is manifested externally instead of what is in the heart. God never judges according to the flesh but according to the spirit.

As we are enabled to see the heart, turning away from judging according to the flesh, we can begin to see value in others, completely contrary to what is manifesting on the outside. Are you beginning to see how this mind of innocence toward others can win the hearts of men? This is not meant to be applied as a *technique*. No, on the contrary, as you begin to develop a heart of innocence, which actually exists within you by the Holy Spirit, that heart will naturally look at others in a new light. And that light of love will shine on their hearts and say to them, "Awake, O sleeper, and rise from the dead, and Christ will shine *on you (also[57])*."[58] Because in the light of love, all fear is cast away, they too will begin seeing themselves as Christ sees them—in love. With this thought in mind, I would like you to read this account from the scriptures. See how beautifully it applies to what I have been communicating here:

---

[57] Implied.
[58] Ephesians 5:14.

At dawn he appeared again in the temple courts, where all the people gathered around him, and he sat down to teach them. The teachers of the law and the Pharisees brought in a woman caught in adultery. They made her stand before the group and said to Jesus, "Teacher, this woman was *taken in the (very) act*[59] of adultery. In the Law Moses commanded us to stone such women. Now what do you say?" They were using this question as a trap, in order to have a basis for accusing him. But Jesus bent down and started to write on the ground with his finger. When they kept on questioning him, he straightened up and said to them, "If any one of you is without sin, let him be the first to throw a stone at her." Again he stooped down and wrote on the ground. At this, those who heard began to go away one at a time, the older ones first, until only Jesus was left, with the woman still standing there. Jesus straightened up and asked her, "Woman, where are they? Has no one condemned you?" "No one, sir," she said. "Then neither do I condemn you," Jesus declared. "Go, and sin no more."[60] When Jesus spoke again to the people, he said, "I

---

[59] Wording from KJV (for effect).
[60] Wording from KJV (for accuracy).

am the light of the world. Whoever fol-
lows me will never walk in darkness, but
will have the light of life." The Pharisees
challenged him, "Here you are, appearing
as your own witness; your testimony is not
valid." Jesus answered, "Even if I testify on
my own behalf, my testimony is valid, for
I know where I came from and where I am
going. But you have no idea where I come
from or where I am going. You judge by
human standards; I pass judgment on no
one. But if I do judge, my decisions are
right, because I am not alone. I stand with
the Father, who sent me. In your own Law
it is written that the testimony of two men
is valid. I am one who testifies for myself;
my other witness is the Father, who sent
me." (John 8:2–18)

Oh, my God! What a beautiful picture of how God
views His Son! Now you may say, "Wait a minute, isn't
Jesus dealing with a woman who had committed adultery?
How can you say this is a picture of how God views His
Son?" Have you read the scripture that says, "When you
have done this to the least of these my brethren you have
done it unto me?"[61] And remember how we have already
said that Christ Himself entered into our very sin and how
God viewed Him as His beloved Son? Well, as we view this
woman found in sin, we see how God deals with both the

---

[61] Matthew 25:40.

woman found in her sin *and* how He dealt with His own Son who was found in our sin. For in God's eyes, they are one. Jesus became one of us, so we could be one with Him. So Jesus looks at the woman and says, "Who is it that condemns you?" And she says, "No one, Lord." Then He says, "Neither do I condemn you." Here we see the heart of the Father toward the Son and the Son toward the woman, as if they are one. He sees her value not in what she has done or not done, but in who she is. He sees not her sin, but the beauty of this woman falsely accused by her brethren. Now one might say, "She was not falsely accused. She was guilty of adultery." Yes, she had committed adultery. They were false accusations in that they came from the hearts of the Sadducees driven by the mind of Adam, evaluating by external appearances and actions but not according to how God sees.

Then Jesus tells the woman, "Go, and sin no more." From a legalist or carnal perspective, this is interpreted, "Go, and quit sinning." From the perspective of grace and truth, it means, "Go, begin walking in *My* view and opinion of you, separated from all sin and loved by God!" Believe me, Christ's concern for this woman was not that she had committed adultery. What Jesus was concerned about was saving her from the lie which enslaved both she and her accusers from a life of striving for life through the knowledge of good and evil. If sin existed in this scenario, it was found in all of them missing the mark. They found themselves believing a lie about themselves and about God. This lie was at the root of these religious leaders uncompassionate actions toward this woman. But Jesus actions and words toward her began communicating to her how God actually viewed her. The belief system of these religious leaders found them accusing and judging based on their knowledge of Good and Evil. This belief system is Satan inspired and does not come from God. Yet it was what they believed. And it is why their hearts were hardened.[62]

As we read this example, we see the perfect picture of a group of religious people. It could really be almost *any* group of religious people. The same lie that dictated the young woman's behavior was also in them, but it was far more deeply entrenched in the hearts of those of the religious mindset. Because they had given themselves over to the belief system that righteousness comes through the law, by their own discipline and efforts, they found themselves given over to iniquity. Seeking to establish their own righteousness in the earth, they found themselves condemning one whom the Son of God had declared innocent. Their hearts were blinded by an erroneous belief system which would not allow them to see the heart of that woman as Jesus did or the fact that she was loved by God. They could only evaluate by external actions and appearances. They looked upon someone loved by God and condemned her. For religion, defined as establishing righteousness by your own overt actions (trying to change yourself), finds its root in the lie.

The best way to see and consider this is to view the woman found in adultery as Jesus and the religious leaders as who they were. Just as they judged and condemned the woman, so they would later judge and condemn the Holy One of God. In this illustration, Jesus uses a woman caught

---

[62] Proverbs 4:23.

in the act of adultery as a picture of Himself (the one who became our sin), for all scripture speaks of Him.[63] Again, which is the greater sin, to have committed adultery or to condemn and kill someone Christ loved more than His own life? I think the answer is obvious!

So here we see these religious leaders actually in deeper sin than the one they are accusing. Their form of judgment and understanding had them view all of life through the eyes of sin. Viewing life in the fashion they found themselves condemning her and waited for God to do the same, and if He didn't act, they were quite willing to do it for Him. Though these religious leaders thought of themselves as servants of God, their actions were the very opposite of God's, for God was in Christ, not condemning but *reconciling the world unto Himself.* Though these religious leaders viewed their own actions as righteous, their belief system actually had them behaving contrary to God. Kind of crazy, isn't it? But we see this every day all over the world.

Yet this is even crazier. Consider in this story how Jesus deals with even these religious leaders from a heart of innocence. He does not respond to them according to the law. Instead he stoops and writes on the ground, on stone. This signifies that He and the Father are one, for Jesus is the very finger of the Right Hand of God. And with that finger, He Himself had written the very law they were professing to obey yet falling far short of it. But instead of condemning them, He stands and says, "If any of you are without sin, let him cast the first stone." In saying this, He was trying to shed light on the reality that they had been misinterpreting

---

[63] John 5:39 – 40

the law and its purpose. For if they had understood, they would not have condemned the innocent. For God desires mercy, not sacrifice.[64] Jesus did not even condemn the religious legalists, completely lost and separated from the life of God as they were. He only wanted them to see the truth, and some began to see; the eldest even unto the youngest.

So what about today? As we look about at the religious world, what do we find? Masses of religious organizations of every sort, some new, some thousands of years old, all the various Christian religions, the Jewish religion, Islam, Hindu, Confucianism, and the list goes on. Yet in all of them there contains one common thread: every single human religion is devised by man and depends on man. The lie of Satan has them saying to themselves, "By my wisdom, my righteousness, by my obedience to the law and to God, *I* will attain salvation and godliness." Religious practice is simply man's attempt to somehow fashion a life for himself that only God can produce in us. They fail to realize that the outflow of love produced by an indestructible life cannot be replicated. It is found in the life of God, and that life is found in Jesus. This life comes from God Himself and is experienced in our lives by faith, as the scriptures say, "The righteous shall live by faith."[65] It is believed by the religious that if *I* can obey the law of Moses, if *I* can follow my religions rules (or the principles of some scriptures), if *I* can learn more, then *I* will be seen as righteous, then *I* will find peace with God and man. But all this is based on the work of man's hands and not on Christ. I

---

64 Matthew 12:7
65 Romans 1:17

need to remind you, the essence of idolatry is the worship of the work of man's hands. Please understand, I am not calling anyone an idolater. I am merely saying that when we approach God with the works of our own hands, it is *as* idolatry. As good as all the self-effort we see in religion may appear outwardly, though there may be a "shadow of truth" found in it all, these works are not of the truth. They actually equate to the actions of idolatry. Yet the God who called you out of darkness into His marvelous light hath said, "Wherefore come out from among them, and be ye separate, saith the Lord, and touch not the unclean *thing*; and I will receive you, *And I will be a Father unto you, and ye shall be my sons and daughters, saith the Lord Almighty."* (2 Corinthians 6:17–19)

A curious thing about that verse: when I first came to believe in Christ, I had a friend quote that to me. His interpretation of what it was saying to him and what he was trying to convince me of was "Come out from among the sinners and no longer do the things they do." My response to him was "I did. *I came out from believing as they do.* But I physically separate myself from no man. Because He has made me a son, I am no longer a partaker with them of the unbelief which motivates their behavior." As little knowledge as I had way back then, the Spirit showed me how my friend's thinking was not exactly right. I understood, even back then, that the "unclean things" the scriptures were speaking of in this verse, were not the sinful things people do, but the things others thought could bring them life. This is all a matter of perception. As the eyes of our hearts become aware of the reality that we have been given an eternal, indestructible life, striving to find life by external religious practices begins to seem quite foolish. Believing this way we can begin to look at life and the things of this life as they were meant to be viewed and enjoyed, but not as something that can possibly be the source of true happiness. As the scriptures say, "To the pure, all things are pure, [66] but to those who are corrupted and do not believe, nothing is pure. In fact, both their minds and consciences are corrupted"[67] To those whose lives have found the fulfillment of life in Jesus, life and the things of this life can be truly enjoyed. But to those who have not come to believe, and to the religious, so much of this life is looked upon as evil. The innocent can view life from a platform of life having been completely fulfilled in us, through him.

As I look out on most Christian religion, I am intrigued. How people can substitute the gift of righteousness, which has been freely spoken to us in Jesus, for their own performance is something I cannot understand. As I speak with so many brothers and sisters in Christ, whose thinking is so performance based, it seems as if their lives are all about what "they are doing for Christ (or what their organization is doing)." No one speaks of Christ and what God has said and done in Him. Neither do I think they even fully understand this. Something is deeply amiss here.

Think about it this way. If God has called you holy and righteous and good and we go about trying to *be* holy and righteous and good, do you not see you are actually fighting against God? For the God we know, is the God who calls things that *are not* as though *they are*, and in this way,

---

[66] Titus 1:15

[67]

they come into existence.[68] Listen carefully. If He called you holy and righteous and good, *you are* holy and righteous and good, period! Simply live your life now in light of who you are—holy and righteous and good and quit fighting God by striving to be that way! Somehow in the heart and mind of man, when we truly believe something is true, it simply becomes that way for us. Faith instills in the heart that which is believed. And from the heart flows the issues of life. Otherwise, we never cease our strivings. The heart that finds itself innocent never strives to find innocence. It simply is innocent. So be innocent!

Since religion is supposedly all about faith, I would like to share with you what faith can do. Jesus said, "If you had the faith of a mustard seed you could say to this mountain, 'Be cast into the sea,' and it would be cast into the sea." Now the carnal mind hears this and believes Jesus wants us to have faith. So it sets out to attain it. The carnal mind then sets out to muster up faith (no pun intended). Or it hears this and says, "Maybe if I pray for faith I can attain it." But this was not Jesus's intent in what he was sharing. What He was saying was that *faith* in the human heart is very powerful, even in the smallest amount. I am personally convinced that if a person believes something about himself, that person quite literally becomes that way, even someone who does not know the Lord. Proverbs puts it this way, "As a man thinketh in his heart, so is he."[69] When a person deeply believes something about him or herself, they conform fully to that image. This is true to

---

[68] Romans 4:17.
[69] Proverbs 23:7.

the point that, if a man believed or thought he were a horse long enough, not even trying to be a horse, people will soon be looking at that guy saying, "Look at that guy! He looks and acts just like a horse." Maybe that is an extreme example, but it is not without a point. Our thoughts and resultant actions are dictated by what we believe.

Our lives are transformed and powered by faith. Since our creation in the image and likeness of God, the ability to believe (faith) has been a part of our human makeup. Even after the fall, this part of our makeup remained completely intact. What we believe dictates how we operate. Our fruitfulness as human beings is affected by the way we operate as dictated by that belief system. The problem is, the belief system found in the world has us believing we need to prove ourselves good or righteous. Attaining that goal is elusive and striving toward it produces unending work, which never ends. But the truth speaks a different word to us. It reveals to us what God has spoken to us in Jesus; *that we are as we should be.*

Man has difficulty separating behavior from person-hood. But as the scripture say, 'Man looks at the outward appearance, but God looks at the heart.[70] In Christ, God is enabling us to see who we are in Jesus. He has separated who we truly are from our mere outward actions. This faith, or belief system comes from God, and is *very good.* This is what the Bible calls salvation through the forgiveness of sins and the 'gift' of righteousness. These words from the apostle Paul testify to this glorious reality.

---

[70] 1 Samuel 16:7.

Brothers, think of what you were when you were called. Not many of you were wise by human standards; not many were influential; not many were of noble birth. But God chose the foolish things of the world to shame the wise; God chose the weak things of the world to shame the strong. He chose the lowly things of this world and the despised things--and the things that are not--to nullify the things that are, so that no one may boast before him. It is because of him that you are in Christ Jesus, who has become for us wisdom from God--that is, our righteousness, holiness and redemption. Therefore, as it is written: "Let him who boasts boast in the Lord." (1 Corinthian 1:26–31 NIV)

Can you see here how, because we are now the children of God and He sees us as righteous, holy, and good, that this is not of us but of Him? He has created us this way by the Word of God (Jesus), who speaks all things into existence.[71]

So to understand where religion is coming from in our day, we must remember that it was the same in Jesus's day. The religious leaders of His day heaped up rules and regulations and principles upon people, tying heavy loads upon the people. Yet these *religious ones* could not see that what they were doing was supplanting the work of God in the lives of their constituents. It is "the blind leading the

---

[71] Psalm 100:3.

blind!"[72] The weights they lay upon others, they themselves cannot even bear. They do not have enough faith to believe that God alone is the transformer of the human life, so they set about fashioning people in the image they think they should be. And oh how good it all looks, externally. All the while God is crying out, "Let my people go!"

This may seem harsh toward religion. But the church has become bewitched and its slumber is deep. As John wrote to the church at Ephesus in the book of Revelation, the church for the most part has left their first love;[73] Christ Himself! They have left Christ as their head and supplanted Him with their own efforts to establish 'churches'. But Christ is the rock on which the church is built. Only through Him does the individual overcome in this world. Yet in the church there is a sense that something is missing. The legalistic, carnal mindset I speak of is pervasive in the professing church today. But instead of finding the answer in the Grace of God that brings salvation to all men, they see grace as the enemy and actually become even more legalistic, bringing death to all men!

I once read an article in a very popular and respected Christian magazine on *legalism*. It was a compilation of articles written by a number of respected Christian writers. Every single article spoke of our being set free from the law. Yet in their description of this, they described our being set free from law in this fashion. "We are no longer under the law! Of course this does not mean we have been set free from the moral law of God, the Ten Commandments, but

---

[72] Matthew 15:10–20.
[73] Revelations 2:4.

from *ritualistic law*. 'For surely the Lord wants us to obey the Ten Commandments.'" So here we find this highly regarded magazine publishing an article supposedly combating legalism yet actually promoting it! To them legalism is something you might find in a Christian religion like Catholicism, where there is much form and ritual seen. But if Paul were speaking of ritualistic law when he said, "You are *no longer under law*, but grace,"[74] then how could he say, "If *righteousness* cometh through the law, Christ died for nothing"?[75]

Righteousness has nothing to do with ritual. A righteous person is one who finds himself possessing a character equal to that of God, with that character producing similar actions[76] Christ has attained this equality for us. He did this by His death and resurrection from the dead. And this transaction is not without effect. It produces within us the fruit of God. *For God is the righteous One, and the only one who can establish righteousness in the human heart.* This is specifically why the prophet Jeremiah would refer to God as 'The Lord *our* righteousness'.[77] When, by faith, a man or woman sees his or herself as clothed with the very righteousness and character of God, both righteousness and eternal life are fully attained. This state of being produces the fruit of God's Spirit in the life of that believer. He or she becomes an overcomer! This righteousness far exceeds the law of Moses—*the moral law of Moses no less!*

---

[74] Romans 6:14.
[75] Galatians 2:21.
[76] The Greek word for righteousness 'dikaiosune' as defined by Strong's-The basis of this statement.
[77] Jeremiah 23:6.

Every believer I know belongs to a religion or a church. I too attend a church. Whether you find yourself a teacher who may have been confused about these things or someone attending a church where legalistic teaching exists, there is great hope. Christ has set us free from forever trying to find life through manipulating things in this life. He did this so that our lives might be moved and motivated by the Spirit. The Spirit becomes active in our hearts and lives as we begin hearing what He is saying to us. And this is what He says—"You have been given everything you need for life and godliness! "You have been set free from sin and are now slaves to righteousness; now controlled by the love of God that is found in Jesus!"[78] What religion can you find that can provide such a thing as this? And if there is a religion out there that is telling you such things, I am *all for* that religion. I attend such a church. Though rare, they do exist! But this is the critical issue. The Spirit of Truth is what establishes the life of God in the human heart. So, finding and allowing *that truth* to be ingrained in your heart and mind is what is needed. Once this truth is found, guard your heart, and refrain from listening to competing spirits.

---

[78] 2 Peter 1:2–4; Romans 6:17–18.

Chapter 7

Darkness Dispelled by Light

To come to a clearer understanding of these things, we need to understand that God's desire is to move us as individuals from a state of darkness to a state of light. This is why you find both darkness and light in the scriptures. Clearly darkness exists in this earth, and clearly there is light. God's purpose is that we not stay in gloom and darkness, but that we move into His glorious light. This state of darkness began when the light of love and innocence was lost in Adam. And this darkness was death to our existence, a blindness that could only be penetrated by the light of life. Death and blindness can only be dispelled by that light of life. For God to make this work, He had to provide for us something far greater than what Adam had, for what Adam had could be lost. Though mankind was created in the 'image of God', the Lord desired something even greater for His children. Something that could secure for them the understanding and completeness that is found in the light of His presence. He had to make them one with Him, married as if it were, to Him. Only in that state could men and women from every nation be truly secure with God for all eternity.[79]

To understand the distinction between the light and the darkness, we need to see what it means to "rightly divide the word of truth."[80] Because the scriptures contain darkness and light, gloom and glory, distinctions between these elements need to begin to take shape in our hearts and minds.

Rightly dividing the word of truth is learning to see which is which. It is our coming to see the darkness from the light. It is also coming to realize that we have been translated from the kingdom of darkness to the kingdom of light. What we find in most Christian theology and teaching today is a blending of darkness and light. This lack of understanding and poor teaching keeps us from experiencing the true light. But to find that distinction, is to step into the light and find yourself both enlightened and enlivened by that light. Listen to these words from the book of Hebrews. It speaks of this very distinction and the glory of one over the other:

> You have *not* come to a mountain *that can be touched* and that is burning with fire; to darkness, gloom and storm; to a trumpet blast or to such a voice speaking words that those who heard it begged that no further word be spoken to them, because they could not bear what was commanded: "If even an animal touches the mountain, it

---

[79] Revelation 21:9.
[80] 2 Timothy 2:15.

must be stoned." The sight was so terrifying that Moses said, "I am trembling with fear."

But you have come to Mount Zion, to the city of the living God, to the heavenly Jerusalem, the city of the living God. You have come to thousands upon thousands of angels in joyful assembly, to the church of the firstborn, whose names are written in heaven. You have come to God, the Judge of all, *to the spirits of righteous men made perfect* [emphasis added], to Jesus the mediator of a new covenant, and to the sprinkled blood that speaks a better word than the blood of Abel.

See to it that you do not refuse him who speaks. If they did not escape when they refused him who warned them on earth, how much less will we, if we turn away from him who warns us from heaven? At that time his voice shook the earth, but now he has promised, "Once more I will shake not only the earth but also the heavens." The words "once more" indicate the removing of what can be shaken—that is, created things—so that what cannot be shaken may remain.

Therefore, since we are receiving a kingdom that cannot be shaken, let us be thankful, and so worship God acceptably with reverence and awe, for our "God is a consuming fire." (Hebrews 12:18–29 NIV)

My god, what a distinction! Some of the words in these writings from Hebrews may seem somewhat fearful; yet the purpose of these writings are meant to alleviate fear, not instill it. In the words of these scriptures, we are being told how God, in Christ, did not bring us to a mountain that "can be touched," a place where the doom and fear of death reigns. In other words, he did not bring us to a physical mountain similar to the one from which the law was given. No, He has taken us to a heavenly mountain full of joy and hope! It is just that, for the moment, those who fear cannot clearly see the distinction between the light and darkness. The letter (that which is of this physical creation) has for them taken precedence over that which is of the Spirit. Prior to the Spirit of God revealing to us His heart, we all initially interpret life and God by a carnal perspective. Yet as the scriptures clearly communicate to us, 'the flesh perishes, but the Spirit gives life.'[81] As the Spirit begins to dispel the darkness in our hearts and reveals light to us, we begin seeing life with a new and clearer vision as hope and an eternal perspective begins to interpret life for us. Let us now begin to shed some light on these distinctions as we leave the darkness behind and find ourselves being clothed in His glorious light.

In order to begin seeing the distinction between darkness and light, we must first come to an understanding of the two great covenants found in the scriptures. We must also see that it is only in dying to one that you can become alive to the other. As human beings, our primary means of understanding is external or carnal. So the only way God

---

[81] 2 Corinthians 3:6.

could begin to relate and communicate to us was in that fashion. So the words of scriptures become clear, "The spiritual did not come first, but the natural, and after that the spiritual."[82] For this very reason God first gave us the covenant of the law. It was instituted by Adam but was shown for what it is on Mount Sinai by Moses, as mentioned in the earlier quotation from the book of Hebrews. The second covenant is the covenant of grace which is found in the Spirit of Jesus.

Now someone might ask, "I thought there were many covenants found in the scriptures? For instance, I have heard of an Adamic Covenant called the Age of Conscience. Was this covenant different than the covenant of law?" The answer to this is no. There is no difference, the only difference is in form. The Adamic Covenant often called by some the Age of Conscience began when Adam fell to a belief system that said, "By my knowledge of good and evil, I will attain godliness (or God likeness)." At that time, this became a law or a principle, entrenched in men's hearts whereby they believed that by their efforts, based on their internal knowledge of good and evil, they could find fulfillment in life. The problem is, the man and woman, nor anyone coming after them, were capable of understanding what had happened to them. This mode of thinking became quite natural to them. As natural as it may have felt to them, as discussed previously, this belief system was death to them. It is the root of all sin. So in God's goodness, He provided us with what was fit for our thinking. He said (this is not a quote, but clearly implied), "Let us give

---

[82]   1 Corinthian 15:46

man a gauge or a plumb line so he can see that his thinking will only lead to sin and death." "Let us give them a very remedial picture of goodness (the Ten Commandments) so they can see that by any form of 'knowledge of good and evil,' they will only find enmity between one another and resultant death." But in the midst of this darkness, He imbedded a dimly lit light, a gauge or a plumb line of another sort—something to provide them with hope. It was the idea that a sacrifice would be provided that would show man his true worth to God apart from his knowledge of good and evil.

Though the sacrificial system was a part of the law, it was very different from the rules and regulations which seemed to be meant to direct human behavior. It said to us, 'If you find yourself incapable of keeping these laws, if you find that by the works of your own hands righteousness cannot be attained, God will provide a sacrifice for you.' In this sacrifice you will come to see your value and worth to God fully apart from your works. This sacrifice was alluded to in various scriptures throughout the Old Testament and is fully revealed to us in Jesus.

The purpose of the law, in an overall sense, was to reveal to mankind their flawed belief system. The ultimate goal of all this was that mankind would seek Him and find their innocence restored through God's Son. So what does man do in response to all of this? Not seeing that dimly lit light, they take the carnal ordinances of the law that were meant to reveal this flawed belief system and turn it into something to be venerated and worshiped. But God was not overcome by this darkness, neither was He surprised by the way they handled the law. He knew men would see the law this way, so He let them strive toward obedience to the law until they could see it simply didn't work, for no one has ever attained eternal life by means of the law. Then, in what the scriptures call 'the fullness of time', God sent His Son into the world. His purpose in doing this was to bring light to our darkness; enabling us to see what our darkened minds were unable to see prior to Jesus coming; His good view and opinion of us. Listen to the apostle Paul here—

> As long as the heir is a child, he is no different from a slave, although he owns the whole estate. He is subject to guardians and trustees until the time set by his father. So also, when we were children, we were in slavery under the basic principles of the world (this flawed mind-set)[83]. But when the time had fully come, God sent his Son, born of a woman, born under law, to redeem those under law, that we might receive the full rights of sons. Because you are sons, God sent the Spirit of his Son into our hearts, the Spirit who calls out, "*Abba*, Father." So you are no longer a slave, but a son; and since you are a son, God has made you also an heir. Formerly, when you did not know God, you were slaves to those who by nature are not gods. But now that you know God—or rather are known by God—how is it that you are turning back

---

[83] Comment by MGC

to those weak and miserable principles? Do you wish to be enslaved by them all over again? You are observing special days and months and seasons and years! I fear for you, that somehow I have wasted my efforts on you. (Galatian 4:1–11)

This is a perfect picture of all mankind. We were children, though owning the whole estate (all that is God's). But we saw ourselves as slaves, evaluating and seeing life through the mind of Adam. Our erroneous perception of the law of Moses chained us as slaves to the very system we thought would bring us life. But the law itself clearly communicates to us that 'this way,' leads only to death. For no one has within themselves the ability to obey the law." The law was meant to connect our external actions (or sinful behavior) to the system of belief that was already in us. In other words, the law of Moses was given to us by God to reveal to us that the way of the knowledge of good and evil leads only to sin and death. This is why Mount Sinai is described as such a fearful place in that passage from Hebrews, and that even touching that mountain would bring death. But in the fullness of time, at just the right time in human history, Jesus was born into the world. His purpose in this was that we would no longer see ourselves as slaves, bound and chained to sin as revealed by the law, but as the very sons and daughters of God because that is who we are! He died to free us from any sense or idea that relationship and fellowship with God could be attained through obedience to the law of Moses or through the work of our own hands.

The idea that obeying laws or principals could possibly establish sonship is utterly preposterous and foolish, for faith and love cannot be found in obedience to external commandments or law.[84] The law was but a shadow of true righteousness. Love is the fulfillment of it. And that love comes to us as we begin seeing ourselves for who we are, the sons and daughters of God greatly loved by the Father. Yet even back in the days when Paul wrote those previously quoted words from the book of Galatians, believers were turning back to worthless laws and principles. The law of Moses represented the very belief system that Christ died to redeem us from! This tendency to return to a law based system is still prevalent in the Christian world today.

When I was a child, I happened to have a great dad, though early on I did not see him exactly that way. I thought he was a stern person. Because I lacked knowledge as a kid, my father had to enforce rules on me simply to keep this ignorant kid from running out into the traffic. I really did not know what I was doing in life (although I thought I did). I was under his tutorship, though an heir to my father's entire estate (small as it may have been). Yet looking back at all of this, I knew there was something behind that sternness, a deep abiding love he had for me which I could not see clearly because I was still under that tutorship. During that tutorship period, I did something really, really bad. I totaled my parents' brand-new car, almost killing myself and a friend. We were both drunk as skunks. Shortly thereafter, my dad came to get me out of jail. When I saw his face, I saw what looked like rage in his

---

[84] Galatians 3:12

face. I said to myself, "Oh my god, I am in for it now." But a strange thing happened. When he saw I was hurt (both in body and spirit), the rage left his face and he said to me, "It's over son. I know you will learn from this." His deep love for me became evident as he completely dispelled any idea that I had done wrong and showed his love and concern for me and my well-being.

I was in bed with an injury that whole summer. Yet I never heard one single negative word from my parents about this issue that summer or for the rest of my life. Their love for me as their son overshadowed any transgression I may have committed. But do you want to hear a curious thing? The dumb young person I was, I did not fully perceive my father's love for me at the time, nor did I really learn my lesson, for I drank and drove many times after that. But as my father had said, somewhere in the deep recesses of my mind I actually did 'learn from this.'

That lesson became apparent to me many years later when I read of God's love for me even though my life may not have been as it should be, or should I say *my actions* were not as they should be.

> You see, at just the right time, when we were still powerless, Christ died for the ungodly. Very rarely will anyone die for a righteous person, though for a good person someone might possibly dare to die. But God demonstrates his own love for us in this: While we were still sinners, Christ died for us. (Romans 5:6–8, NIV)

As I read those words, the incident with my father almost immediately came to my mind. It helped me to easily see how a deep abiding love from God can actually exist though my actions may have been fully out of the way. At that very point, so many years after that incident, I finally realized just how much my daddy truly loved me. This is an apt example of how God fulfills the law in the heart of a human being. He took what was written in stone, the command to "honor your father and mother," off of stone, and placed that love in my heart toward them!

It's a beautiful thing to see God taking our personal experiences, combining it with the Spirits ability to enlighten, bringing forth love in our hearts. He knows where we are, He knows exactly what we need and He is with us in the midst of it all. As the Lord begins to reveal to us that it is His deepest desire to give us all things, our hearts can begin to know what true security actually looks like. Listen to these beautiful words from the apostle Paul, as he expresses these very things to us:

> Let no man deceive himself. If any man among you seemeth to be wise in this world, let him become a fool, that he may be wise. For the wisdom of this world is foolishness with God. For it is written, He taketh the wise in their own craftiness. And again, The Lord knoweth the thoughts of the wise, that they are vain. Therefore let no man glory in men. *For all things are yours; whether Paul, or Apollos, or Cephas, or the world, or life, or death, or things present, or*

things to come; all are yours; and ye are Christ's;
and Christ is God's. (1 Corinthians 3:19–23
KJV, emphasis added)

What Paul is saying here is an old and repeating story. There were those back then, and there are those today, who would have you striving to attain righteousness through following religion's laws and principles. A system that seems comfortable and safe, but leads nowhere. Do not give in to them. For you are Christ's. You are a son or daughter of the God of this universe. So much so that the angels of heaven long to look into these things. The angels themselves long to understand what has been freely given us in Jesus.[85] And all things belong to you! All the truths given us by Paul and Peter and the others are yours. The whole world is yours. The life found in this world has no power over you, for even life and death are yours. We have no fear of the future, not even of present things or the things to come. For they are yours! What in the world else could a human being possibly need?

There is simplicity found in Jesus and the covenant of grace. In this relationship God simply gives you everything you have been striving for but never able to attain. In this covenant we live, and move and find our existence as it was meant to be, for—

If there had been nothing wrong with that first covenant (the covenant of law)[86], no place would have been sought for another.

---

[85] 1 Peter 1:10–12.
[86] Comment by MGC.

But God found fault with the people and said: "The time is coming, declares the Lord, when I will make a new covenant with the house of Israel and with the house of Judah. It will not be like the covenant I made with their forefathers when I took them by the hand to lead them out of Egypt, because they did not remain faithful to my covenant, and I turned away from them, declares the Lord."[87]

"This is the covenant I will make with the house of Israel after that time," declares the Lord. "I will put my laws in their minds and write them on their hearts. I will be their God, and they will be my people. No longer will a man teach his neighbor, or a man his brother, saying, 'Know the Lord,' because they will all know me, from the least of them to the greatest. For I will forgive their wickedness and will remember their sins no more." By calling this covenant "new," he has made the first one obsolete; and what is obsolete and aging will soon disappear. (Hebrews 8:7–13 NIV)

The law was a shadow of the truth, not the reality of it. Though the scriptures contain the Word of God, their purpose is to point us to the reality of the person who is the true Word of God, Jesus. For it is through Jesus that light is

---

[87] Insert from KJV.

shed on God's true heart and intentions toward mankind. The Word of God is more than a compilation of books written in ink on paper containing a body of information. And contrary to how many view the Bible as a 'guidebook for life', seeing the scriptures this way, blinds you to its true intent and message!

During His earthly ministry Jesus made a statement well worth consideration. This statement illustrates for us how the truth eludes those seeking to intellectually understand the scriptures. He told the religious leaders of His day, "You study the scriptures diligently because you think that in them you have eternal life. These are the scriptures that testify about me, yet you refuse to come to me to have life"[88] These religious leaders were deeply into the scriptures. They studied and memorized them, probably more than most of the theologians of our day. Yet they completely missed the very one of whom the scriptures were pointing to. Because their hearts were bent on the establishment of their own righteousness, they missed the righteousness that comes from God as a gift. Through their own intellectual efforts toward understanding, they missed the Spirit of the scriptures only seeing the letter. But unlike the Pharisees, we, with unveiled faces can see and reflect the One who is our righteousness. This is "Christ in you the Hope of Glory"[89]

When we think of the idea of the 'Holy Spirit', or the 'Spirit of God', it is important to note that though the Spirit is an integral part of who God is, there is also disposition

---

[88] John 5:39–40.
[89] Colossians 1:27.

towards us found in that Spirit. This disposition speaks to our hearts, revealing to us our sonship, revealing to us who we are to Him. It says to us "I love you and I always have. You are my son or daughter, for you know me as I truly am! I no longer attach any sin to your account. My Spirit within you both provides and reveals to you your oneness with Me, and that same Spirit will provide for you all the love, joy, peace, patience, kindness, and longsuffering you have ever dreamed of."[90] This eternal flow of life within us has given us eternal life and one day will one day provide us with an incorruptible physical body just as Jesus has. It is this life from God, not some external commandments, which now animates our lives. This Spirit of the law now resides in our hearts by which He enables us to see God as He truly is, a loving father, as Abba!

The law of Moses is only in keeping with the Spirit in that a sacrifice would atone for sin and provide for life, but the carnal ordinances themselves could never produce life. They only demand the flesh to perform, having us forever longing to be clothed with glory and immortality. Now that we have been so clothed, we find ourselves no longer under the law. If there is a law today, it is the law referred to by the apostle Paul which he calls the "law of the Spirit of life." This law makes foolish the wisdom of the world, which wants to establish righteousness by personal efforts. The Spirit of life eliminates all striving and produces the fruitfulness that can only be initiated in the human heart at rest.

The highest form of human life, the greatest quality of life that can be experienced, is found in that place where

---

[90] John 17:20–23.

sincere love begins to well up in your heart toward God spontaneously. As this love fills your heart, it overflows to everyone around you. You think to yourself, *Where does this overwhelming love I feel for everyone come from?* And as you consider this you realize, "My God, it is not just for those who treat me well, and it is not just for those whom I know personally. This love permeating my life is for everyone!" And in this overflow of love, you find yourself desiring to be a friend to those around you. Not in any sense of obligation or duty, but because in your heart, in a very natural way, you simply desire to be.[91] This is where life finally becomes good, really good!

The law of Moses speaks to the world. It tells us that life is not found in our knowledge of good and evil, for in it we find ourselves bound to a life which continually finds itself at enmity with God and men. It reveals to us that our carnal way of thinking leads only to death. However, there is a Word spoken to us in Jesus. That Word dispels all this darkness and gloom and provides us with the light of truth. This truth speaks a word to us, saying, "These are my beloved children in whom there is no guile, only innocence."[92] As we believe this message, innocence is brought to life in our hearts by the Spirit. And in that life, the darkness which once clouded our view and proper perspective of God and His love for us, is dispelled by light; the light of His glorious life!

---

[91] John 7:38.
[92] John 1:44–51.

Chapter 8

The Essence of Forgiveness

Growing up as a child, I was taught a concept of forgiveness which is pretty much universally taught in the world in which we live. It really does not matter which religion you belong to or who the human teacher is. The general idea is this. We all sin. This angers God and creates a barrier between He and us. This condition results in a lack of fellowship with God, requiring forgiveness from God. In essence, we see ourselves at enmity with God due to some bad behavior, and something needs to take place to make it right. The form of how we 'get it right with God' may vary. Confession and repentance from sin is probably the most popular, as seen in the evangelical Christian world. Among other groups you see other things; self-sacrifice, deep remorse, fasting, etc. But with regular, fairly un-religious people, we just see people doing good deeds to others in an effort to make up for their shortcomings or to somehow make up for what they may have done wrong.

In all of this we have got to stop and ask ourselves a simple, yet very serious question. Are any of these means of forgiveness according to the truth we find in Jesus? What

is true forgiveness, and what does it mean to be truly forgiven? To come to grips with the answer on this, we need
to understand the relationship between the One who *is*
forgiveness and the ones who *are forgiven!* In all of human
history, there is one example of forgiveness which stands
above them all. Listen to this story; in all the world there
is none better. For it speaks a clear word to us of how God
relates to man and sees them as forgiven. Jesus tells this
story:

> "There was a man who had two sons. The
> younger one said to his father, 'Father, give
> me my share of the estate.' So he divided
> his property between them.
>
> "Not long after that, the younger
> son got together all he had, set off for a
> distant country and there squandered his
> wealth in wild living. After he had spent
> everything, there was a severe famine in
> that whole country, and he began to be in
> need. So he went and hired himself out to
> a citizen of that country, who sent him to
> his fields to feed pigs. He longed to fill his
> stomach with the pods that the pigs were
> eating, but no one gave him anything.
>
> "When he came to his senses, he
> said, 'How many of my father's hired men
> have food to spare, and here I am starv-
> ing to death! I will set out and go back to
> my father and say to him: 'Father, I have
> sinned against heaven and against you.

I am no longer worthy to be called your son; make me like one of your hired men.' So he got up and went to his father.

"But while he was still a long way off, his father saw him and was filled with compassion for him; he ran to his son, threw his arms around him and kissed him. The son said to him, 'Father, I have sinned against heaven and against you. I am no longer worthy to be called your son.'

"But the father said to his servants, 'Quick! Bring the best robe and put it on him. Put a ring on his finger and sandals on his feet. Bring the fattened calf and kill it. Let's have a feast and celebrate. For this son of mine was dead and is alive again; he was lost and is found.' So they began to celebrate.

"Meanwhile, the older son was in the field. When he came near the house, he heard music and dancing. So he called one of the servants and asked him what was going on. 'Your brother has come,' he replied, 'and your father has killed the fattened calf because he has him back safe and sound.'

"The older brother became angry and refused to go in. So his father went out and pleaded with him. But he answered his father, 'Look! All these years I've been slaving for you and never disobeyed your orders. Yet you never gave me even a young goat so I could celebrate with my friends. But when this son of yours who has squandered your property with prostitutes comes home, you kill the fattened calf for him!'

"'My son,' the father said, 'you are always with me, and everything I have is yours. But we had to celebrate and be glad, because this brother of yours was dead and is alive again; he was lost and is found.'" (Luke 15:11–32 NIV)

This is an extremely interesting and captivating story, and not without reason. For in this story we see a perfect picture of how God views all of mankind and the true nature of His forgiveness toward them. As we touched on earlier, there is a vast difference between the letter of what the scriptures say and the depths of truth contained in what the Spirit is capable of revealing to us.

As we look at this story, consider how in the midst of the younger sons adventures (or better said misadventures), he was always somehow aware of his father's love for him. Yet somehow he was lured away from that love by thoughts of a better life elsewhere, a life he could fashion for himself by the work of his own hands. So he goes off to a far country and squanders his inheritance on wild living and prostitutes. But things go desperately awry. This form of life was found by him to be useless and void and his life falls apart. Then, at some point, he comes to his senses.

His heart remembers the life he had left, and he returns to his father to be less than a son (at least in his own mind). Now the father, unbeknownst to this son, never stopped thinking of him as a son. So before the son even says a word to his father, while still at a great distance, his father sees him and feels great compassion for him. He runs to his son, throws his arms around him, and kisses him. Then the son says to him, "I have sinned against heaven and against you. I am no longer worthy to be called your son." But the father, *contrary to what the son had said (not because of it, as some would tell you),* tells his servants, "Quick, bring the best robe and put in on him. Put a ring on his finger and sandals on his feet. Bring the fattened calf and kill it. Let us have a feast and celebrate. For this son of mine was dead and is alive again, he was lost and is found."

The fathers love toward the son had always been alive. It was just that the son had not seen or truly experienced that love for himself. But when that love became evident to him, the truth of it all overwhelmed his heart, joining his heart to the heart of the father in love. This is forgiveness and how forgiveness is experienced! Forgiveness is that place were someone who should be offended by your actions, is not offended. It is a place where someone who should hate you because of what you have done only holds love and compassion in their heart towards you. This is pictured beautifully in this story; and it is a perfect picture of Gods forgiveness towards us. God's nature is to love and show His loving kindness towards us.

Then a curious thing happens in the story. After the father and the son's fellowship had been fully restored, there came a sacrifice. This is very peculiar, for we are often taught that forgiveness comes to us *because of* a sacrifice, not before a sacrifice. But true forgiveness is not the satiation of anger due to a sacrifice. It was the sacrifice itself which revealed the love that was always there; the sacrifice coming after love is revealed in celebration and the culmination of the two coming together as one. It is as if, though the love had always existed, the sacrifice is what seals and signifies it; it reveals to us its existence. Just as at the cross, God in Christ forgave all, even the ones crucifying him, *before* his death. He then gave his life as a fragrant offering to the father for the ones He loved as a testimony to the Father of his love for us. Thus, we see the fulfillment of scripture which says, "Without the shedding of blood, there is no forgiveness." Without Christ's death, love would never have been realized. God, in Jesus, literally signs his covenant of love for us in His own blood, testifying the two have become one (He with us), having placed His own robe on us. We are now clothed by Him in His resurrected life!

Now the elder son was incensed, angry at this vulgar display of love to someone so unworthy! After all, he had been *working* for his father all this time! In fact, he was in the fields working when all this took place. But as he communicated his disdain for all of this to his father, did the father chastise him? No! he says this, "My son, you have been with me, and everything I have is yours. But it is right to make merry and be glad. For this thy brother was dead and is alive again; he was lost and is found." Yet this son would not enter in to the fathers feast. Here we see how even a legalistic belief system is met with compassion and love by a loving father. Yet the mind set on the flesh would not enter.

These two young men present to us a picture. The one son, seeing and experiencing the forgiveness which was found in the father's heart of love toward him apart from his sin, the other believing that by his works he could attain good standing with the father. In doing so he completely missed seeing the love and forgiveness that was found in the father. The elder son found himself bound to a life apart from intimacy with the father; forever striving through life, jealous of the one who found rest in His father's love for him. All humanity is camped out in one of these two belief systems, but the Father holds out forgiveness and healing in his wings to us all. And so Jesus cried out,

"O Jerusalem, Jerusalem, you who kill the prophets and stone those sent to you, how often I have longed to gather your children together, as a hen gathers her chicks under her wings, but you would not." (Matthew 23:37 NIV/KJV)

The Jewish nation (as a whole) and the rest of the religious world are all seeking to establish *their own* righteousness and godliness, and they seek forgiveness by their own sacrifices. Sadly, they seem never to truly find either: righteousness or forgiveness. For righteousness and forgiveness are not things to be worked for, or even sought after; it is something that came to us! God pursued us. He gave us these things in Jesus, that we might see that they were in Him all along.

Simple minded men tend to find the truth easy, while the wise and prudent sift through all the religious and philosophical mire, seeking but often never finding it. This is why the proverbs say, "He giveth understanding unto the simple."[93] This is why Paul would later say, "The wisdom of the world is foolishness to God. For it is written, 'He taketh the wise in their own craftiness.'" Putting aside your own wisdom and understanding is the key to finding that you are already forgiven. As Moses told the people at the Red Sea, "Fear ye not, stand still (work not), and see the salvation of the Lord. The Lord shall fight for you, and ye shall hold your peace."[94] Finding the eternal peace of God comes through the cessation of work and resting upon the work of God at the cross, where Jesus did no work but trusted in the love of the Father. He knew He was loved and that God would raise Him from the dead. Jesus's life blood spilled out on the ground, testifying to His faith in God.

As we come alive to the truth that the Father's love toward Jesus is the same love He holds toward us, we recognize and come alive to that forgiveness. Forgiveness is not a thing to be attained. It is a place to reside. We live and move and have our being in the state of being forgiven. This reality, when it comes to rest in our hearts, builds within us the firm foundations of faith, hope, and love. Where these things are present, moving in the human heart, the need to purposely forgive others is eliminated. For when faith, hope and love dwell in the heart, all men appear forgiven to you. Forgiveness becomes the natural outflow of our lives when we find ourselves not holding anything against others.

---

[93] Psalm 119:130.
[94] Exodus 14:14 KJV.

We are taught that we need to forgive others as some overt act on our parts. But the ultimate purpose of God was that we possess a forgiving spirit. As usual man takes what was meant to be a part of the natural outflow of the human spirit and makes it into a work. Doing so, we negate the heart of it all and find ourselves forgiving, while still harboring bitterness in our hearts. This is what happens when you are just *'performing'*. But when we see ourselves *'as forgiven'*, forgiving becomes natural and real. Not only is this so, but knowing you are forgiven begins building godly character in one's own heart. Listen—

> His divine power has given us everything we need for life and godliness through our knowledge of him who called us by his own glory and goodness. Through these he has given us his very great and precious promises, so that through them you may participate in the divine nature and escape the corruption in the world caused by lust.[95] For this very reason, make every effort to add to your faith goodness; and to goodness, knowledge; and to knowledge, self-control; and to self-control, perseverance; and to perseverance, godliness; and to godliness, brotherly kindness; and to brotherly kindness, love. For if you possess these qualities in increasing measure, they

---

[95] This word from KJV denoting a coveting of something one does not have.

will keep you from being ineffective and unproductive in your knowledge of our Lord Jesus Christ. But if anyone does not have them, he is nearsighted and blind, and has forgotten that he has been cleansed from his past sins. (2 Peter 1:3–9 NIV)

Peter is reaching out to us, imploring us to continue in the truth which says, *"We have been cleansed from our past sins."* The God who called us *by* His own glory and goodness *into* His own glory and goodness desires nothing more than for us to rest in the completeness that is ours in Christ. Peter reiterates to us that fruitfulness and effectiveness in life are fully dependent on our hearts being established in the forgiveness that is ours, and how that fruitfulness is somehow stymied in the heart which has forgotten that it *has been cleansed from its past sins.* I love how the King James Version uses the term *"purged* from his past sins." And this is exactly what has happened, God in Jesus has *purged* us from our past sins. So the question is, how many of our sins are in the past? All of them! And yet we have some people telling us that we have not been purged, that God is still counting our sins against us, and that we still need to do something to expiate (or get rid of) our sin. Can you see how the truth stands in stark contrast to the lies we have been taught?

So why is it so important to know you have been purged of your sins? When we believe sin encumbers our fellowship with God, we are actually operating in unbelief. Fellowship with God exists by faith. By faith in what? By faith in the reality that we have been completely purged from our sins once for all time! Believing that fellowship with God exists by your own doing negates the very work of God and establishes in our hearts a lie which has us continually questioning our stance and acceptability to God. If you believe that lie, you will forever be dealing with and trying to overcome sin, never truly feeling the ability to approach God with freedom and confidence[96] and you will never feel as though you are one with God. Yet, as we have previously stated, being made one with Him was the very purpose of Jesus coming to us; and in Him is no sin.[97]

True fellowship with God is found in coming to the realization that the same glory and honor and immortality that is found in God, is now fully attributed to you. Seeing yourself this way, forgiveness no longer becomes something to attain to, but a state you find yourself in. This is that place where you find no attachment to sin; the forgiveness of God finding its perfect work in you. This is the mind of Christ Himself. But sadly, contrary to all this, we see what is taught in most churches: you are 'not forgiven', you have to confess your sins, and in doing so you can somehow overcome sin. Yet the apostle Paul, contrary to this philosophy, said just the opposite. He said, "Forget what is past and press on toward those things which are before."[98] What are *these things*? It is all the riches and treasures of wisdom and knowledge which are found in Christ! Forever remembering your sin leads to a miserable life where you can never

---

[96] Ephesians 3:12.
[97] 1 John 3:5.
[98] Philippians 3:13.

find rest. There is another way. Listen to these words from the writer of Hebrews:

"Then I (Jesus)[99] said, 'Here I am--it is written about me in the scroll—I have come to do your will, O God.'"

First he said, "Sacrifices and offerings, burnt offerings and sin offerings you did not desire, nor were you pleased with them" (although the law required them to be made). Then he said, "Here I am, I have come to do your will." He sets aside the first to establish the second. And by that will, we have been made holy through the sacrifice of the body of Jesus Christ once for all.

Day after day every priest stands and performs his religious duties; again and again he offers the same sacrifices, *which can never take away sins.* But when this priest had offered for all time *one sacrifice* for sins, he sat down at the right hand of God. Since that time he waits for his enemies to be made his footstool, because by one sacrifice he has made perfect forever those who are sanctified[100]. The Holy Spirit also testifies to us about this. First he says: "This is the covenant I will make

[99] Implied.
[100] From KJV.

with them after that time, says the Lord. I will put my laws in their hearts, and I will write them on their minds." Then he adds: "*Their sins and lawless acts I will remember no more.*" *And where these have been forgiven, there is no longer any sacrifice for sin.*

Therefore, brothers, since we have confidence to enter the Most Holy Place by the blood of Jesus, by a new and living way opened for us through the curtain, that is, his body, and since we have a great priest over the house of God, let us draw near to God with a sincere heart in full assurance of faith, having our hearts sprinkled to cleanse us from a guilty conscience and having our bodies washed with pure water. Let us hold unswervingly to the hope we profess, for he who promised is faithful. (Hebrews 10:7–24 NIV, emphasis added)

Let me put this as blatantly as I can, for this is of supreme importance. The idea that you are NOT *completely* forgiven and made holy once and for all time is a lie. These scriptures, as well as many others, testify to that truth. Those who teach that we are not completely forgiven at all times are in serious error, yet they are simply passing down what they have been taught. This idea is steeped in legalism where you find yourself forever sinning, confessing, and repenting. That cycle will never end, and sweet fellowship with God cannot begin until we hear the truth and believe.

You are a son or daughter of God, in whom He is well pleased completely apart from your actions. God has separated you from your sin once and for all. He has fully sanctified you. He has taken you out of your sins and placed you into Christ. If God had to do anything more to remove sin from you, Jesus would have to come down to earth again and die for your sins again, but He will not! His was a once-for-all sacrifice and was fully sufficient and completely effective. Your sins have been taken away; they no longer exist. Knowing this forgiveness in your heart enables you to finally understand the words of John the Baptist, as he uttered these words as he first looked upon Jesus; the only words necessary to utter of Him, "Behold the Lamb of God, who takes ways away the sin of the world!"[101]

I know someone might say in response to all of this, "Well we still sin. What do we do with those sins?" The answer to this is *nothing!* Just believe what God has said about them. Believe He has taken them away. When you screw up and do something wrong or hurtful to someone else, it is only the heart that knows that Jesus has taken away our sin, that can truly be sorry and apologize (and that with a clear conscience). Any other form of forgiveness will either forgive out of some sick sense of obligation, or requiring something of others in order to forgive them. This form of forgiveness is not from God, but based on our being required to do so; your own self-effort. No one will ever see the love of God in such a thing. But because we

---

[101] John 1:29.

are the beloved sons and daughters of God and have been made partakers of the divine nature,[102] these words are now true of us:

> That all of them may be one, Father, *just as you are* in me and I am in you. May they also be in us so that the world may believe that you have sent me. I have given them the glory that you gave me, that they may be one as we are one: I in them and you in me. May they be brought to complete unity to let the world know that you sent me and have loved them even as you have loved me. (John 17:21–23 NIV)

How much closer to God can we possibly be? The fellowship with God people so deeply desire and strive for has been fully accomplished for us. We experience this fellowship as we begin seeing the very spirit that was in Him, having forgiven us, freely expressing itself in us—forgiving others. Forgiveness and fellowship with God are not things to do, they are something that happens to you. Fellowship does not come through what we do. It is not found in reading in the Bible, prayer or through the good things you do. These things are not the essence or source of true fellowship. We are in Him and He is in us; *this is fellowship!* He is the one who works in us to will and to do that which is His good pleasure.[103] The things His Spirit moves in our

---

[102] 2 Peter 1:4.
[103] Philippians 2:13.

hearts to do, whatever that might be, are the only things we need to see manifested in our lives. And love is always the motivator of these activities. Otherwise they are worthless; like a clanging cymbal.[104]

Fellowship with God is found in knowing you exist in the presence of God, fully known and fully forgiven. Jesus died to secure this for you. Do not let anyone teach you or convince your heart of anything less. The desire of the enemy of your soul is that you see yourself somehow provisionally forgiven. Anyone teaching this is not doing God's work; and their error is not trivial. You are completely forgiven and fellowship with God is yours! Any other teaching is from the spirit of the Antichrist; the propagator of the lie. From what I can see, he is doing a pretty good job in this world. But oh, how good it is to be forgiven!

---

[104] 1 Corinthians 13:1.

Chapter 9

Life as a Son

I have heard folks say, "We are all the children of God." And there is some truth to that statement, but what it means to be a son or daughter of God is far more meaningful than first meets the eye. There is a difference between having been fashioned in the image and likeness of God and being a Son. Every human being, in a very real sense, is the offspring of God. Listen to these words from the apostle Paul and how he describes God and our unique relationship with Him as human beings.

> Paul then stood up in the meeting of the Areopagus and said: "Men of Athens! I see that in every way you are very religious. For as I walked around and looked carefully at your objects of worship, I even found an altar with this inscription: TO AN UNKNOWN GOD. Now what you worship as something unknown I am going to proclaim to you.

"The God who made the world and everything in it is the Lord of heaven and earth and does not live in temples built by hands. And he is not served by human hands, as if he needed anything, because he himself gives all men life and breath and everything else. From one man he made every nation of men that they should inhabit the whole earth; and he determined the times set for them and the exact places where they should live. God did this so that men would seek him and perhaps reach out for him and find him, though he is not far from each one of us. 'For in him we live and move and have our being.'

"As some of your own poets have said, 'We are his offspring.' *Therefore since we are God's offspring, we should not think that the divine being is like gold or silver or stone- -an image made by man's design and skill.* In the past God overlooked such ignorance, but now he commands all people everywhere to repent. For he has set a day when he will judge the world with justice by the man he has appointed. He has given proof of this to all men by raising him from the dead." (Acts 17:22–31 NIV, emphasis added)

Most people's understanding of 'being a child of God' is identical to that of these Athenian philosophers to whom Paul was conversing with in these passages. They somehow innately knew there was some connection between them and their creator. But they had not yet come to know Him, or the truth of His thoughts, disposition or intentions toward them. Paul acknowledges this to be true. Without question, mankind holds a very special position above all of the rest of creation. But there was something missing; some kind of disconnect. This disconnect had these searchers searching. Though they longed to be seen as sons, they never knew Him in any intimate fashion. And though they desired a deep meaningful relationship with God, their believing that relationship was attached to their behavior inhibited their ability truly know God.

So how and when does that Father-son or Father-daughter relationship come into being? Where, in our hearts and minds, do we truly begin to see ourselves fully connected to the One in whom we were so fashioned? In order to see this connection, we need first to see that He does view us as His children and not as just another part of His creation. Somehow, His thoughts toward us need to become our thoughts. As lost as we thought we were, God never stopped thinking of us as His sons and daughters. It was our hearts and minds that went astray, not His. Being a son or daughter of God means that the Spirit and disposition of Christ has become our spirit and disposition. This all comes into fruition as God's Spirit persuades our hearts that the same passionate love the Father held toward Jesus is the same passion and love He holds toward us. Jesus fully knew that after experiencing suffering and death at the hands of carnal minded men and the law system, that God would raise Him from the dead. He knew this because He knew He was the Son of God, loved by the Father. But Jesus was also the Son of man. Jesus brought God down to earth to join Him with man. So, He became our High Priest, and as our Hight Priest (or our representative), we can know that as it goes for Him, so it goes for us!

Jesus died at the hands of sinful, carnal minded men and their belief system. In doing so he became our representative, because we too were under the sentence of death under that belief system. So when Jesus died to that system, because He is our representative, we too died to that system. In this very way we died to death, and death no longer has mastery over us. For anyone who has died is dead to death. So when Jesus, our representative, was raised from the dead, so were we! And now, because our representative Jesus is seated at the Fathers right hand above all rulers and authorities to reign forever, we can see ourselves seated there with Him in glory.[105]

As these truths become intrinsic to who we are, we begin seeing ourselves as more than just a creature fashioned in the 'image and likeness of God'. Deep down in our hearts we are enabled to see ourselves for who we were actually created to be – the very son or daughter of God Himself. Seeing yourself this way causes the Spirit of 'The Son' to begin manifesting Himself in you. God loves you, just as He loved Jesus, and as every good father desires nothing but the best for their child, so God desires nothing but the best for you.

---

[105] Ephesians 2:4–6.

As the Spirit of a son begins developing in your heart, it begins to naturally impart to you a spirit and disposition toward others that has you operating from a heart of innocence toward yourself, toward others, and toward God. This enables you, as a son (or daughter) of God, to live from the passions of the heart rather than the dictates of carnal thinking; free from being required to do things as a slave would.[106] This platform of existence and life is what is known as the law of the Spirit of life. No religion, no form of righteousness by law, no good deeds can produce such a life. In Jesus, we died to such means and walk in His pure sweet love for us. This Spirit enlivens the hearts of men and causes them to come into the fullness of who we were actually created to be. This is what it means to be born of the Spirit.[107] And that Spirit is not without effect. It reveals to us our sonship and provides for us the security that can only come from knowing yourself as a dearly loved son or daughter of God.[108]

Let me give you an example of this from the scriptures. At a critical point in His earthly ministry, Jesus stood in the temple of God and declared this of Himself: "The hour has come for the Son of Man to be glorified. I tell you the truth, unless a kernel of wheat falls to the ground and dies, it remains only a single seed. But if it dies, it produces many seeds." Though Jesus was the very Son of God, He found Himself in human form just as we find ourselves. There were certain limits to His power and influence in the earth. These limits were voluntarily assumed by Him

---

[106] Galatians 4:7–9.
[107] John Chapter 3
[108] Romans 8:14–16.

while in a body of flesh. But as Jesus says here, "The hour has come for the Son of Man to be glorified." Glorification and the fruitfulness of life had to come through death. Just as it requires that a seed fall to the ground and die in order for that seed to sprout and produce much fruit, so it is with the Son of Man and so it is with those born of Him. Just as in Adam all died, so in Christ all must be made alive.[109]

Something happened in Adam that affected all humanity. We found ourselves alive to a life principle, an approach to life or belief system which is called the *law of sin and death*. This belief system finds us striving all the days of our lives in an effort to find life. We believed that peace and happiness came to us by our own "knowledge of good and evil." Not only did Adam partake of that belief system, but we all have.[110] This belief system is so pervasive in the earth that we all find ourselves naturally gravitating to it. We believe, just as Adam did, that we are not a son, or that we were rejected as a son. It is as if, in our minds, we believe He sees us in sin and can no longer look upon us. So this *becomes our reality*. If you ever wonder why people run the other way when God is mentioned, I just shared it with you. After leaving the childlike innocence we possessed as children, we tend to develop an unhealthy fear of God and His truth. This is quite often driven by things we are taught about God that are simply not true. None the less, just as Adam feared God and hid from Him, our natural tendency, initially, is to fear and hide. But this reaction is not based on truth. It is based on our own erroneous belief system.

---

[109] 1 Corinthians 15:22.
[110] Romans 5:12.

Opposed to all of this, we see Jesus. He is described as 'the author and perfector of faith'.[111] Now one might say, "How can this be?" "How can this individual both define what faith is, and perfect it at the same time?" Consider this. Unlike Adam, Jesus believed the father's testimony toward Him, that He was His beloved son. In believing this, he became the author of 'our faith'. At the cross Jesus gave us an alternate belief system to believe in. Adam chose to believe that He could *attain* life by his knowledge of good and evil through his own efforts. Completely contrary to this we see Jesus. *He did nothing to save Himself, but fully trusted in God's love for Him; trusting by faith that His Father would save him by raising Him from the dead. This is the faith he authored for us!* As we come to believe in the Father's love for us, apart from our works, just as we have seen in Jesus, we too are saved and raised from the dead, just as Jesus was!

Jesus was strengthened by the *Spirit of faith* to endure the cross. Likewise we too are strengthened by that same Spirit of faith to handle anything this world has to offer. This indwelling Spirit of faith is what the scriptures refer to as the 'law of the Spirit of life'. It is as if we find ourselves standing in the garden again with a choice, believe in your own knowledge of Good and Evil for life, or believe in the faith of the Son of God. Jesus is the Tree of life! Believe in Him and you become the possessor of eternal life!

The Spirit of faith produces in us a heart that is one in spirit, mind and intent with the creator of the universe. In every sense of the word, we are the children of God.

---

[111] Hebrews 12:2.

Intimacy with God is now not only possible, but the natural result of being made one with Him. We have been make perfect in relationship with God. As the scriptures say, 'For by one sacrifice he has made perfect forever those who are sanctified.'[112] This word 'perfect' is interpreted by some as complete. But in its context, the English word 'perfect' is the perfect word to use (no pun intended!). For His sacrifice has completely done away with sin as it relates to us. Now we can see ourselves as God sees us; restored to innocence and perfection. In our hearts we are being transformed into that likeness as we grow in our understanding and awareness of this reality.

In some beautiful way, because we are the children of God,[113] He is building His kingdom of perfection and innocence in our hearts. God has gifted every man and woman a measure of faith innate within them to believe.[114] Everyone has the capacity to believe. The proper use of faith is simply seeing what He has done for us and accepting it as sufficient for your complete, eternal salvation. In doing so He glorifies us as His children, and Himself as the One who is just and the justifier of everyone who has faith in Jesus![115]

---

[112] Hebrews 10:14.
[113] 1 John 3:2.
[114] Rom 12:3.
[115] Romans 3:26.

Chapter 10

Death to the Law for Life

There is both an outward superficial side of truth and there is a spiritual side. It is not that the outward and superficial (or carnal) understanding is useless until something far better takes its place. When something far better does come along, the carnal and superficial becomes useless and obsolete,[116] for the spiritual fully reveals what was once only seen on the surface. This is especially true as we look at the religious world's understanding of the law, specifically the law of Moses, which we commonly think of as the Ten Commandments.

What I have been writing about may cause some to say, "Man, this is great! Now I really know who I am. Just as Jesus was the Son of God in whom the Father was well pleased, so am I! I am one with the Lord, the creator of the universe! Everything that is His is mine, and I now have the mind of Christ! What a revelation!" But inevitably, this is the next question that comes up. *"What do I do now?"*

---

[116] Hebrews 7:19.

This is a very common and understandable question and from a carnal perspective seems to make sense to us. But the question itself is rooted in misperception. It is rooted in the lie. To approach life with this question in mind will actually bring death, and religion feeds you with answers to this question as if it were actually the correct question to be asked! But these are carnal thoughts which do not come from God. As this question comes to your mind, you must remember this, you are not a human *doer*, you are a human *being*. Somehow, even in human language, God has interposed this truth to us. Just as God is not a doer (though He has done much), so were we meant to 'be', or to 'exist' and function in the same way He functions. Just as He *exists* as "I am," and that life has produced much, we need to learn to exist in love and allow His life to produce its fruit. Though our flesh cries out for a direction manual, we can say, "No! I am who I was created to be, and He loves me as I am!"

From a biblical or scriptural perspective, there are those who might understandably say, "What about Paul's writings? Are there not instructions to the believers found in his writings about human activity?" I am going to give a concise answer to these questions, then afterward go on to discuss the law of Moses and its purpose in the world.

First, I would like you to imagine something. Imagine you died. Imagine you were no longer in the weak body of flesh in which we now live. Imagine you were in heaven with the Lord, right now. You would be there, your spirit would be there, but because you would be absent from the body of flesh in which we now live, things would be quite different. Your existence would simply be your spirit infused with the life of God. Perfection would have come to your personal being, completely apart from the weakness found in the flesh. And when the Lord would return, you would return with him, and in the twinkling of an eye, your physical body would be raised incorruptible and glorified as it met your spirit in the air. Thus, or in this very state, you will forever be with the Lord.[117] So this is the question. At that point, do you believe you would need some law or instruction book to tell you what to do? Anyone with a head on their shoulders would have to answer, "Of course not! If all were made perfect and our flesh done away with, my life and thoughts and actions would be one with the Lord's, exactly as they should be."

Let's take this a step further. God's desire for us is that we not operate from external instruction or influences whatsoever but that our hearts be motivated solely by His indwelling spirit of innocence. As we come to see more and more of His good view and opinion of us and the reality that He has always felt this way toward us, that very spirit begins to well up within us, producing love. This love is the fulfillment of the law and becomes the motivator of all human activity. At this point, every need for external instruction fades to needlessness. This is the very place in life He desires us to be.. Though many are just finding this way, it is, nevertheless, the way! Listen to these words from the apostle Paul as he speaks of this very thing.

> *Love never fails.* But where there are prophecies, they will cease; where there

---

[117] 1 Thessalonians 4:16–17.

are tongues, they will be stilled; where there is knowledge, it will pass away. For we know in part and we prophesy in part, but when perfection comes, the imperfect disappears. When I was a child, I talked like a child, I thought like a child, I reasoned like a child. When I became a man, I put childish ways behind me. Now we see but a poor reflection as in a mirror; then we shall see face to face. Now I know in part; then I shall know fully, even as I am fully known. (1 Corinthians 13:8–12, emphasis added)

What Paul is describing here as he says, "When perfection comes, the imperfect disappears" is not what it will be like when we get to heaven (although there may be some application to that). The perfection he is speaking of is the perfection of love. For in love we find fullness of life, and this fullness can never fail us. All the gifts, the instructions, the prophecies, and special knowledge, everything Paul often speaks about fades to nothing as we peer into that mirror, looking at ourselves, and as that image clears, we see Him. Coming to know this love which surpasses all knowledge, we are transformed into His image with ever-increasing glory.[118] Consider this. Isn't it a preposterous thought to think any external rule, ordinance, or principle can provide this level of existence? God is moving us into the light of this understanding right now. But early on

---

[118] 2 Corinthians 3:18.

in our understanding, because we do exist in the weakness of a body of flesh, we need a description of this life. All the special gifts and the instructions given us by Paul are for this very reason. Until we begin to see the treasure and perfection which is held in these earthen vessels of ours (our bodies), these instructions may be necessary. But when the love of God found in Jesus begins to supplant the weaker means for guiding human activity, we find that love fully sufficient for the motivation of every human behavior and for life.

Remembering that there is more to the scriptures than first meets the eye, a spirit behind the words, listen with spiritual ears these instructions from the apostle Paul. Once the spirit of the instruction is grasped, the spiritual takes precedence over the carnal instruction and the need for any carnal instruction fades to nothingness. So Paul says, "Husbands love your wives." Listen to this instruction closely. It is communicating to us an amazing truth:

> Husbands, love your wives, *just as Christ loved the church and gave himself up for her to make her holy, cleansing her by the washing with water through the word, and to present her to himself as a radiant church, without stain or wrinkle or any other blemish, but holy and blameless. In this same way, husbands ought to love their wives as their own bodies. He who loves his wife loves himself. After all, no one ever hated his own body, but he feeds and cares for it, just as Christ does the church—for we are members of his body. 'For*

this reason a man will leave his father and mother and be united to his wife, and the two will become one flesh.' This is a profound mystery--but I am talking about Christ and the church. However, each one of you also must love his wife as he loves himself, and the wife must respect her husband. (Ephesians 5:25–33, emphasis added)

In what Paul is communicating to us here he says, "Husbands, love your wives." But his explanation of this is not some detailed instruction on "how husbands are to love their wives." Instead he presents to us a picture of Christs' love for us. Not as some 'how to' example. Paul understood that in speaking of Jesus' love for us, love would somehow be born in our hearts toward our wives. As we see the beauty He beholds in us, this reality speaks to us deeply of our oneness with Him and with one another. This is why He would picture the marital relationship as "a profound mystery." Paul's spiritual exposé on the love between a man and a woman has to begin with Christ's love and union with us. This spiritual description takes a simple instruction and infuses the love of Christ into it. These spiritual instructions speak love into our hearts, causing it to become natural for a man to love his wife and natural for a woman to respect her husband.

I know this may be a hard saying, but God can help you see this. As this Spirit of love and innocence begins to permeate our hearts, loving others in a very deep and passionate way begins to require no external means or manipulation to occur. Love is not something we are instructed or commanded *to do*, it is something that either exists or does not exist in the heart of a man or woman. Jesus's intent and purpose in His life, death, and resurrection to glory was to infuse that love into our hearts by the Spirit which lives in us. This love causes us to love people; it creates in us a new heart.[119]

Let me illustrate it to you this way. How would you feel if your wife told people, "I love my husband because I was commanded to and because I am being obedient to God"? Though someone might say, "That's nice," for me I am personally hoping for much more from my wife. What I am hoping for is to experience the reality of a deep, passionate love she holds for me, welling up from within her toward me. Think about it. There is a stark difference between the cold letter of the law demanding love, and having a spirit of love. This is specifically why Paul told us not to go back to the law for life.[120] The reality of love experienced is infinitely greater than that which is manipulated into being by some command or instruction.

So one might ask, "What about the law of Moses so esteemed in the world as being the way to righteousness, do we just do away with it?" The simple answer to this is "Of course not." If the whole world were infused with life, there would be no need or purpose in the world for the law of Moses. But this is not the case at the present time. The world misinterprets the nature and purpose of the law of Moses. They believe the law of Moses is what brings righteousness to men, but they are seriously wrong.

---

[119] Ezekiel 36:25–28.
[120] Galatians 2:19–21.

So what then is the purpose of the law if it cannot bring about a true, internal goodness that emanates from the heart? The law of Moses was meant for one ultimate purpose—to reveal sin. I am not speaking of what is traditionally considered sin, the fruit of the flesh, though it does that also. When I speak of sin here, I am speaking of a belief system—the system which today motivates the hearts of every human being on earth. This lie, believed on in the world, is what brings about all other forms of visible sin and the resultant death. The law does but one thing. It reveals to us the lie upon which we have been basing our existence; that through our knowledge of good and evil, godliness (or God likeness) could be attained.

Because this lie so permeated the thinking and reasoning processes in the human heart, God said, "Let me show to them that this way, is not *the way*, and will only lead to death." So He gave us His law from Mount Sinai. And for over three thousand years, no one has obeyed it, though many have valiantly tried. Everyone lies, everyone covets; no one loves God with their whole heart and soul and mind. The law does not bring about righteousness, it only exposes the fact that through human effort we will never attain it! It teaches us by the deeds of our flesh, we can *never* attain godliness! The scriptures teach us that *this way*, the way of the knowledge of good and evil, leads only to death. In fact, it is what brings death to the entire human race!

Jewish history is filled with bondage, slavery and death, yet they tenaciously hold on to the law as if it will save them. It is not that God made these things happen to them, neither did the law itself cause this, for there is nothing wrong with the law itself. But because the people believed that the law system (or their knowledge of good and evil) would save them, they experienced that life of bondage and death. But God's intention was to reveal to that nation, and through them the whole world, that the way of the knowledge of good and evil is not the way; but instead is rooted in pride, self-justification and unbelief. He said, "Let me reveal to them, through the law, that this belief system will only produce enmity between human beings and that death would be the result." And so the Jewish nation throughout human history has found itself at odds with all the nations around it. And they never *became righteous* as the result of the law.

God's ultimate purpose was to use the Jewish nation to reveal this human condition to the whole world. Yet God, even in the midst of the Jewish nation's misunderstanding, has always loved this peculiar people—and He loves us as well. Our only salvation from an endless cycle of sin and death is to believe the truth of the "really good news of the gospel," which is completely contrary to the law. It says that God loves us completely apart from our efforts to find righteousness through our knowledge of good and evil or our ability to obey the law. It says the life we so desire, *eternal, immortal, everlasting life*, is given to us freely apart from our works or effort and regardless of sin. This is why the scriptures clearly say, "Where sin abounded, grace did much more abound!"[121] The peace of God, and the rest that is found in Him, is only attained as we cease our own work and find our rest in His love for us.[122]

---

[121] Romans 5:20.
[122] Hebrews 4:10.

What happened to Jesus at the cross perfectly illustrates to us this reality. God took a man who knew no sin. Another way to say this, is that He abided in innocence. Yet the world treated Him as if He were full of sin, for they crucified Him naked on a tree, as if He were some vial offender. They said to Him, "If thou be the Son of God, come down from the cross." And they hurled other abuses at Him, saying, "He trusts in God. Let God rescue him now if he wants him, for he said, 'I am the Son of God.'" [123] He became our representative as He hung there. The world saw Him through *their own eyes*, yet God saw Him through His eyes. Coming in the likeness of sinful flesh and experiencing the ridicule of sinful men, He *bore* our sin in Himself, as if *we* were hanging there on the cross. But in the midst of our sin, God did not abandon or reject Him. When Jesus said, "My God, My God why have you forsaken me," he said it for the benefit of the people. It was as if he were crying out in all the pain and confusion of all humanity, dying in their sin, saying, "Lord, have you forsaken me in this place?" Yet Jesus knew the truth of God's love for Him would triumph, for love triumphs over judgment. [124]

In that cry, He was saying, "Have you really forsaken me Lord? Lord, show them your love for Me and for them in not abandoning your Son to the grave." Many in that crowd knew the psalm Jesus seemed to be quoting—Psalm 22—as he uttered those words, "My God, My God why have you forsaken me?" It is important to note that Jesus is not quoting a psalm; the psalm, being prophetic, was actu-

---

[123] Matthew 27:43.
[124] James 2:13b.

ally quoting Him! This psalm, written long before Jesus came to this earth, reveals to us the depths of the heart of Jesus as He found Himself hanging there on the cross. It goes on to clearly communicate to us that God had not abandoned his Son, neither did the Son really believe He had been abandoned. In fact, as He hung there, Jesus was fully trusting God. Jesus said and did all these things to prove to us that in the midst of our sin, God had not forsaken *Him*, neither will He forsake *us* in our sin! These events prove to us that God loves us apart from our knowledge of good and evil or our efforts to prove ourselves by the work of our hands. Listen to these words written by David—Psalm 22, which fully proves the reality of what I am saying. These words were written a thousand years before it happened, proving its validity.

> *My God, my God, why have you forsaken me?* Why are you so far from saving me, so far from the words of my groaning? O my God, I cry out by day, but you do not answer, by night, and am not silent. (Clearly how Jesus felt while being rejected by men and how men feel toward God)[125] Yet you are enthroned as the Holy One; you are the praise of Israel. In you our fathers put their trust; they trusted and you delivered them. They cried to you and were saved; in you they trusted and were not disappointed. But I am a worm and

---

[125] Comment by MGC.

not a man, scorned by men and despised by the people. All who see me mock me; they hurl insults, shaking their heads: "He trusts in the LORD; let the LORD rescue him. Let him deliver him, since he delights in him." Yet you brought me out of the womb; you made me trust in you even at my mother's breast.

From birth I was cast upon you; from my mother's womb you have been my God.

Do not be far from me, for trouble is near and there is no one to help. Many bulls surround me; strong bulls of Bashan encircle me. Roaring lions tearing their prey open their mouths wide against me. I am poured out like water, and all my bones are out of joint. My heart has turned to wax; it has melted away within me. My strength is dried up like a potsherd, and my tongue sticks to the roof of my mouth; you lay me in the dust of death. Dogs have surrounded me; a band of evil men has encircled me, they have pierced my hands and my feet. I can count all my bones; people stare and gloat over me. They divide my garments among them and cast lots for my clothing.

But you, O LORD, be not far off; O my Strength, come quickly to help me. Deliver my life from the sword, my precious life from the power of the dogs. Rescue me from the mouth of the lions; save me from the horns of the wild oxen. I will declare your name to my brothers; in the congregation I will praise you. You who fear the LORD, praise him! All you descendants of Jacob, honor him! Revere him, all you descendants of Israel! *For he has not despised or disdained the suffering of the afflicted one; he has not hidden his face from him but has listened to his cry for help.* (Jesus true belief in the Father's love toward him)[126]

From you comes the theme of my praise in the great assembly; before those who fear you will I fulfill my vows. The poor will eat and be satisfied; they who seek the LORD will praise him—may your hearts live forever! All the ends of the earth will remember and turn to the LORD, and all the families of the nations will bow down before him, for dominion belongs to the LORD and he rules over the nations. All the rich of the earth will feast and worship; all who go down to the dust will kneel before him-- those who cannot keep themselves alive. Posterity will serve him, future generations will be told about the Lord. They will proclaim his

---

[126] Comment by MGC.

righteousness to a people yet unborn—for he has done it. (Psalm 22 NIV, emphasis added)

What can you say to such words? Just as Adam believed the lie and so became the representative of all mankind, all believing that same lie, so Jesus believed the truth of God's love for Him. Thus Jesus became the second Adam (or representative) of all mankind. Just as in Adam all died to a life of innocence, believing that God had rejected them and finding themselves bound to a life of striving, so in Christ we are fully restored to a life of innocence before God. This innocence results in a life of peace and rest before God and man!

In each human heart there is a choice—believe as Adam and continue to strive, or believe in Jesus and enter into your rest. The correct choice is obvious. The law of Moses was meant only to reveal to us that a life of striving to attain righteousness by our own efforts is futile; that it is tiring and ends only in self condemnation and death. But true goodness, innocence and even eternal life itself is a gift, not to be worked for, but to receive by faith. Paul puts it this way:

> *There is* therefore now no condemnation to them which are in Christ Jesus (in His mind and spirit),[127] who walk not after the flesh, but after the Spirit. *For the law of the Spirit of <u>life</u> in Christ Jesus hath made*

---

[127] Comment by MGC.

me free from the law of sin and death. For what the law (of Moses)[128] *could not do,* in that it was weak through the flesh, God sending his own Son in the likeness of sinful flesh, and for sin, condemned sin in the flesh: *That the righteousness of the law might be fulfilled in us,* who walk not after the flesh (or the Law),[129] but after the Spirit. For they that are after the flesh (or the law)[130] do mind the things of the flesh; but they that are after the Spirit the things of the Spirit. For to be carnally minded *is* death; but to be spiritually minded *is* life and peace. (Romans 8:1–6 KJV, emphasis added)

Believing the law of Moses or any other religious law is the way to righteousness is rooted in pride. For it says, "I will!" True righteousness reveals itself in the individual finding himself or herself *being loved.* When this reality comes to the human heart, we find ourselves stunned with the reality that, though we believed the law was the way, it is a weak substitute for the thing that takes its place—love.

There is nothing wrong with the Law of Moses; at least not what it *says.* What the law says is good, and holy and true. But as we pursue the law as if it were a means of attaining righteousness, it is as if we are saying in our hearts, *"I will* ascend above to the heights and take my place above the

---

[128] Comment by MGC.
[129] A Reference to Isaiah 14:12–13.
[130] Comment by MGC.

stars of God!"[131] It is as if we are saying, "I will be like God through my knowledge of good and evil." But understand this; both these means and the attitude are not of God. They come from the enemy of our souls!

Jesus came to save us from this false means of salvation, with its life of self-exaltation and strife. Simply put, He took the Spirit of God and placed Him in the hearts of those who believe in Him. This causes us to be innocent; knowing we are loved and filled with God Himself.

In order for us to come alive to God in this way, we need to die to that which we were enslaved to.[132] We have to die to an external form of righteousness so as to be made alive to another form. Listen as the apostle Paul explains:

> Do you not know, brothers—for I am speaking to men who know the law—that the law has authority over a man only as long as he lives? For example, by law a married woman is bound to her husband as long as he is alive, but if her husband dies, she is released from the law of marriage. So then, if she marries another man while her husband is still alive, she is called an adulteress. But if her husband dies, she is released from that law and is not an adulteress, even though she marries another man.

---

[131] Isaiah 14:13–14.
[132] Romans 7:4

So, my brothers, you also died to the law through the body of Christ that you might belong to another, to him who was raised from the dead, in order that we might bear fruit to God. For when we were controlled by the sinful nature (the flesh),[133] the sinful passions aroused by the law were at work in our bodies, so that we bore fruit for death. But now, by dying to what once bound us (sin as revealed by the law),[134] we have been released from the law so that we serve in the new way of the Spirit, and not in the old way of the written code. (Romans 7:1–6)

How much clearer can it be stated? Because we died with Christ (to the system of exalting one's self) and have been raised to life (a life of trusting God's love for us), we are no longer under the law, period! Putting yourself back under the law is putting yourself back under the power of sin founded in the knowledge of good and evil. This is the very thing Christ died to save us from! Don't let anyone, no matter how good their intent is, put you under external guidance for life; for as these scriptures testify, "You died to the law through the body of Christ." We need to divorce ourselves from the law system for life. The idea that we are not under the law, as Paul states in the scriptures is true, but these verses from Romans should be urgently consid-

[133] KJV.
[134] Comment by MGC.

ered. Not only are we being told that we are not under law, but that we need to "*die to the law!*" We who have believed need to consider ourselves dead to the law for life! Listen to these scriptures as Paul explains these things to us. I have interjected some definitions that may help you hear clearly what he is trying to communicate to us:

> For if we have been planted together in the likeness of his death (death to and at the hands of the law system),[135] we shall be also *in the likeness* of *his* resurrection (resurrection to a life of innocence and love):[136] Knowing this, that our old man is crucified with *him*, that the body of sin (striving)[137] might be destroyed, that henceforth we should not serve sin. For he that is dead (to a life of lack)[138] is freed from sin (for we have been provided everything pertaining to life and godliness).[139] Now if we be dead with Christ, we believe that we shall also live with him: Knowing that Christ being raised from the dead dieth no more; death hath no more dominion over him. For in that he died, he died unto sin once: but in that he liveth, he liveth unto God. *Likewise reckon ye also yourselves to*

---

[135] Comment by MGC.
[136] Comment by MGC.
[137] Comment by MGC.
[138] Comment by MGC.
[139] 2 Peter 1:3.

be dead indeed unto sin (and the law which exposes sin),[140] *but alive unto God through Jesus Christ our Lord.* Let not sin (effort to find life by the works of your own hands, through the knowledge of good and evil)[141] therefore reign in your mortal body, that ye should obey it in the lusts (we lust over that which we lack, but God hath provided us everything) thereof. Neither yield ye your members *as* instruments of unrighteousness unto sin (or works resulting in sin):[142] but yield yourselves unto God, as those that are alive from the dead, and your members *as* instruments of righteousness (a life of innocence and love)[143] unto God. (Romans 6:5–13 KJV)

To simplify all this, Paul says to us, "Reckon (or consider) yourselves *dead to sin.*" Even a carnal, superficial understanding of this statement is far better than no understanding at all. Believing this one simple truth would revolutionize the lives of most believers. Think about it. Did anyone ever tell you that you are dead to sin? This idea literally frightens most in religion. "You can't tell people that!" Listen carefully. The business of most religion is to free you from the very thing you are already dead to! Can you see how the idea of telling people they are *dead to sin*

---

[140] Comment by MGC.
[141] Comment by MGC.
[142] Comment by MGC.
[143] Comment by MGC.

might impinge upon their business? They cannot tell people this, even though it is the foundational truth of the gospel itself. But frankly, I do not care about religion. What I care about is people being set free from a life of strife, being provided a life of freedom and peace.

But because Jesus finished work seems to threaten the legalistic religious system, they turn the Grace of God into sin itself, telling people that if you teach grace, you are giving people a license to sin![144] It is as if someone truly found a cure for cancer, but the pharmaceutical companies knew they would go completely out of business if everyone knew of the cure. Do you believe they would really be pushing that final cure? Think about it. Yet unlike some unscrupulous pharmaceutical company pushing drugs, which might help a little; religion doesn't even offer something to help. Instead they often feed the flames of sin in an effort to manipulate human behavior through the external means of the law. This is like a pharmaceutical company giving you a pill that has a little something in it that actually gives you cancer. This may sound like a crazy thought, but in terms of comparison, they equate well.

The apostle Paul made a statement that cannot be overstated. It is simple, concise and meaningful. He said, *"The power of sin is the law."*[145] It is not that law is sin. Mankind was not initially designed to live according to the flesh, but according to the spirit, from the heart. The law, with its external commands and ordinances, is designed to cause us to operate from the flesh, according to our knowledge of

---

[144] Jude 1:4.
[145] 1 Corinthian 15:56.

good and evil apart from the Spirit of promise. Paul puts it this way,

> What shall we say, then? Is the law sin? Certainly not! Indeed I would not have known what sin was except through the law. For I would not have known what coveting really was if the law had not said, "Do not covet." *But sin, seizing the opportunity afforded by the commandment, produced in me every kind of covetous desire. For apart from law, sin is dead.* (Romans 7:7b–8)

The law in any form ties (or binds) us to the very sin we seek to escape. This is specifically what the law was meant to do. Most in religion will never tell you "you are dead to sin," but rather puts you under the very law that feeds it!

So what does it mean to be "dead to sin?" When Adam and Eve came to see themselves as lacking, they set about to clothe themselves with whatever they could find. They chose fig leaves, something that easily decays and is prickly. This is obviously figurative of the way all men have sought to clothe themselves ever since, by their own efforts as determined by their own sense of good and evil. This feeling of lack within them compelled them to clothe themselves. They said to themselves unconsciously, "Man, what can I do to fulfill these deep feelings of need within me, this emptiness?" Because of this perceived lack, we see all the *sinful actions* of men that have ever existed—men and women forever trying to fulfill their needy feelings by the things they do. Then we see the law looking at many of these efforts, telling us that they are sin, because they are not of faith. What a predicament! Here we find ourselves forever trying to satisfy a spiritual need in external ways, by the works of our own hands. At the same time, we find ourselves trying to save ourselves from the very things we are trying to clothe ourselves with, through obedience to the law of Moses. In other words, "*Don't do* the very things you actually believe you *need to do* to clothe yourself." This is a decaying and very prickly process.

Performing the deeds of the law becomes the ultimate in fig leaves, an inadequate means of clothing ourselves with what we believe comes to us from God. But God stepped in at the cross and said, "No! I will reveal to them that I have always viewed them as my sons and daughters and clothe them in my righteousness (or my life). I will show them my good view and opinion of them. They will then see themselves as fully sufficient, lacking nothing. For they will be clothed in immortality and find their union in me! They will become heirs of all I possess; partakers of an eternal kingdom for all eternity. My Spirit within them will convince them of all of this, thus they will find themselves dead to sin!

> For when the time had fully come, God sent his Son, born of a woman, born under law, *to redeem those under law*, that we might receive the full rights of sons. Because you are sons, God sent the Spirit of his Son into our hearts, the Spirit who calls out, "*Abba*, Father." So you are no longer a slave, but a son; and since you are a son, God has made you also an heir. Formerly,

when you did not know God, you were slaves to those who by nature are not gods (external works for life).[146] But now that you know God—or rather are known by God—how is it that you are turning back to those weak and miserable principles? Do you wish to be enslaved by them all over again? You are observing special days and months and seasons and years! I fear for you, that somehow I have wasted my efforts on you. (Galatians 4:4–11)

Coming to believe these truths causes the Spirit of the Son to rise to life within us, the Spirit of the one who loved us and gave Himself for us. As we begin to see ourselves that way, the spirit cries out within us, "Abba, Father! He loves me! He loves me! I am His son!" The only law we need is to be fully enveloped and clothed with His love and the person of Christ Himself. Listen to these beautiful words from the book of Malachi, "But for you who fear my name,[147] the sun of righteousness will rise with healing in His wings. And you will go free, leaping with joy like calves let out to pasture."[148] This is the only way to find true life. Living free requires a death. Death to the idea that you lack, death to finding salvation through the law, and death to self-effort. This is where the resurrected life of Christ begins to produce in you a life you never dreamed possible.

---

[146] Comment by MGC.
[147] Comment by MGC.
[148] Malachi 4:2.

Chapter 11

Free to Be Who We Are

A man is not free when he feels in his heart a need to perform. Yet that feeling exists in the hearts of every human being. In fact, it has been there so long, most people do not even realize it is there, though some certainly may. It is believed if we perform well enough, we will attain the things that will make us happy. This is the driving force behind the lie in the world and its mode of operation, and has become quite natural to us. The problem is, unconsciously, all this effort to appear as something we are not takes a toll. We find ourselves working our way toward something in which we will never find fulfillment, unconscious as that effort might be. We think to ourselves, *If I look this way, people will be attracted to me. If I act this way, they will respect me. If I behave this way, people will look up to me.* Unfortunately, when we are not met with the responses we expect, we become suspect of ourselves and of others. Either something is wrong with me or wrong with them. There is a way to escape this endless cycle of failure and judgment of both ourselves and of others.

Man works for approval or reward, to get something out of it. After all, why would we go through such great effort if there were not something waiting at the other end? God, however, requires no man's approval or reward, for God is fully complete and as He should be. This is why He refers to Himself as I AM. God lacks for nothing, though He desires much. God's greatest desire is for you to be fully complete, even as He is. Though the scriptures say all things were created by Him and for Him, everything He created was meant for us! It gave God great pleasure to freely give us all things, even our very life and breath. And now He has even given us Himself. He did this by revealing to us that we can find ourselves in Him. Our true nature and purpose in life is exposed to us as we come to understand that we are one with Him having been united with Him in His death, burial and resurrection to glory. Understanding this, we find ourselves in Him, seated with Him in glory. And from this platform, we can view life from a completely different perspective. We can be as He is, lacking nothing and desiring much.

So how do we explain this idea of work, and how men find themselves striving all the days of their lives seeking love and approval? Consider here how Jesus addressed the ideas of 'work' and 'rest' with religious leaders of his day. Jesus had just healed a man on the Sabbath who had been a cripple for thirty-eight years, and the Jewish religious leaders wanted to kill him for working on the Sabbath.

So Jesus says to them, "My father always works, to this very day, and I too am working."[149] The Jewish leaders were

---

[149] John 5:17.

under the impression that God's work was finished after He had created all things and at that point He had rested from all His activities. They thought that it was at that point God told man, "Okay, I did my work, now it is up to you. But I will give you a day of rest once a week, so you can rest from all your labors." But their understanding of these events fall short. Though God was very much finished with His work of creation, He never ceases activity. God is an ever-living being, and His life is always productive. God constantly loves. He always protects. He always believes the best of you and is always looking to your best interest. He is always caring about you. He is always patient and kind toward you. He never takes into account your wrongs or scrutinizes your behavior. On the contrary, he serves you with His life. God looks upon those of lower stature than Himself as if they were better than Him, more important than Him. This is the nature of God and was clearly seen in His Son who is the full revelation of God, the exact representation of His being. The apostle Paul tells us that this same attitude, which was in Christ, should be in us.[150] God is working until this very day, revealing truth to us by His Spirit, that we might possess that spirit ourselves. There is rest found in this form of work, for this work requires no effort. It is just God being who He is.

This is where coming to grips with work and the cessation from working gets kind of crazy. God finished His work of creating all that is on the sixth day, the seventh day he rested. But Jesus said, "My father is always working." What does he mean "He ceased His work," and yet "He

---

[150] Philippians 2:1–4.

works always?" How do these two integrate, and where is the application for us in all of this? In this strange contradiction, we find a wonderful truth that empowers us to simply be who we are; no effort, no work, but great fruitfulness. This is a life where true liberty and freedom become reality! Both today, and in the past, God used the Jewish nation as an example to the rest of the world. The Jewish mind-set, which is a little different from the rest of the world, is that both godliness and eternal life itself comes to us through our own work or efforts. They believe, as we do, that to be good and avoid evil behavior will result in salvation for us—all based on some internal or external standard. So God used these people to reveal to us the exact opposite is true.

A very long time ago, there was a promise made to the world which came to us through the prophets' writings. David longed for it when He said, "Create in me a pure heart, O God, and renew a steadfast spirit within me." And Ezekiel foretold its coming,

> I will take you out of the nations; I will gather you from all the countries and bring you back into your own land. I will sprinkle clean water on you, and you will be clean; I will cleanse you from all your impurities and from all your idols. I will give you a new heart and put a new spirit in you; I will remove from you your heart of stone and give you a heart of flesh. And I will put my Spirit in you and move you to follow my decrees and be careful to

keep my laws. You will live in the land I gave your forefathers; you will be my people, and I will be your God. I will save you from all your uncleanness. I will call for the grain and make it plentiful and will not bring famine upon you. I will increase the fruit of the trees and the crops of the field, so that you will no longer suffer disgrace among the nations because of famine. (Ezekiel 36:24–30)

This passage from Ezekiel is deeply spiritual. Prior to Jesus's death and resurrection, no one; neither the Jews, Jesus's disciples, not even the prophets themselves truly understood these things. As you consider what it says, remember. He is not speaking of physical stone hearts or famines related to food or the fruitfulness of trees. Ezekiel is revealing to us that there is a spirit that would be made available to all mankind, which would motivate us by love, causing us to be extremely fruitful. This could not be spoken to them plainly because they did not have Jesus's death for them to interpret it through. Upon Jesus's resurrection to glory, that spirit was poured out toward all men. When the message of God's unconditional love and acceptance of us finds our hearts as individuals, our eyes are opened; His Spirit becomes our Spirit. This is when and how we become one with Him.

God possesses certain thoughts and intentions in his heart toward mankind; very good thoughts and intentions. These thoughts were shared between the Father and the Son by a shared Spirit that was in them. God's greatest desire for mankind is that we too would share the same Spirit that was in them. It is only in 'possessing that Spirit' that we could possibly see and understand those thoughts and intentions. Listen to these words which come to us from the very heart and Spirit of God, as Jesus shares with us what those thoughts and intentions actually are. Listen also to the wording used here. How he uses the terms 'we' and 'our'. They illustrates to us that these thoughts and intentions were shared, and are meant to be shared:

> Verily, verily, I say unto thee, We speak that we do know, and testify that we have seen; and ye receive not our witness. If I have told you earthly things, and ye believe not, how shall ye believe, if I tell you *of* heavenly things? And no man hath ascended up to heaven, but he that came down from heaven, *even* the Son of man which is in heaven. And as Moses lifted up the serpent in the wilderness, even so must the Son of man be lifted up: That whosoever believeth in him should not perish, but have eternal life. For God so loved the world, that he gave his only begotten Son, that whosoever believeth in him should not perish, but have everlasting life. For God sent not his Son into the world to condemn the world; but that the world through him might be saved. (John 3:11–17 KJV)

There is but one thought and intention in the heart of God and that is for you to experience His thoughts and intentions toward you. This is that intention: "I did not come to condemn anyone, but to give eternal life to all." For in Him is found no condemnation, only eternal life. Before Jesus's death and before anyone had really understood God's intentions, John said this of Him, "Whosoever believeth in Him should not perish, but have everlasting life." But to those who *have believed* upon that spirit, it reads, "I will never perish. I have eternal life." So we see the spirit that goes out from God has the same powerful effect on those who believed on it.[151]

Back in the day, when the Spirit was first given to men, a new life sprang up in the earth. It is called *the church.* The church is not an organization, but an organism; people from every nation who have found their eternal life in Jesus. They have found themselves one with Christ, and one with one another, through the common Spirit that indwells them all. This life is easy; for in it you find yourself just being you, no longer manipulating and searching to find life, for you already possess it! No religious organization or law can provide a human being with such completeness. The Lord describes the blessedness of this state of existence as Paul describes the church in this fashion: "The fullness of Him who fills everything in every way.[152]

Shortly after all this had first taken place, some of those among the Jewish believers began to cause doubt to rise within that group. They began to say that in addition

---

[151] 1 John 9–12.s
[152] Ephesians 1:22–23.

to believing in Jesus, one must also obey the law of Moses and perform other religious laws. So the writer of Hebrews addressed this issue. In doing so, he clarifies to us where ultimate freedom and liberty are found. In freedom we find a confidence which enables us to be who we are. This is what he writes to those being led away into this error. These words are from the NIV translation. I have intermingled with my own (but blatantly apparent) explanations:

> Therefore, since the promise of entering his rest still stands, let us be careful that none of you be found to have fallen short of it (short of what—*rest*).[153] For we also have had the gospel preached to us, just as they did (both in Old and New Testament times); but the message they heard was of no value to them, because those who heard did not combine it with faith (for the heart of God, revealed in Jesus, had not yet been seen by men).
>
> Now we who have believed enter that rest, just as God has said, "So I declared an oath in my anger (not anger at them, but their stubbornness),[154] (then God simply declares a truth that)[155] 'They shall never enter my rest (at least not in that way).'" And yet his work has been finished since the creation of the world. For some-

---

[153] Comment by MGC.
[154] Comment by MGC.
[155] Comment by MGC.

where he has spoken about the seventh day in these words: "And on the seventh day God rested from all his work." And again in the passage above he says, "They shall never enter my rest." It still remains that some will enter that rest, and those who formerly had the gospel preached to them did not go in, because of their 'unbelief'.[156] Therefore God again set a certain day, calling it Today, when a long time later he spoke through David, as was said before: 'Today, if you hear his voice, do not harden your hearts.' For if Joshua had given them rest, God would not have spoken later about another day. There remains, then, a Sabbath-rest for the people of God; for anyone who enters God's rest also rests from his own work, just as God did from his. *Let us, therefore, make every effort to enter that rest, so that no one will fall by following their example of unbelief*[57] (Hebrews 4:1–11 NIV)

Let me explain. God's work of creation was finished at the foundation of the world. Everything God created was good and complete. Innocence and fellowship with God reigned on the earth. But our imaginations, carried away by the lie of Satan, spoke a word to us, telling us

---

[156] KJV.
[157] KJV.

that we lacked, that we fell short. So in our hearts and minds, this is exactly what happened; we saw ourselves as having fallen short. We believed God had abandoned us. As a result, we began *working* to rectify these feelings of lack and endeavored to reestablish a relationship with God through the work of our own hands. Yet these *works* manifested themselves in ways contrary to the desires of our hearts. They yielded loneliness and lack. Those feelings we try to fill with everything the world and the law defines as sin. So God did this strange and wonderful thing. Just as God rested on the seventh day from His work, having created everything innocent and good; so on the seventh day, Jesus rested from his work on the cross. Here we see Jesus reestablishing innocence in the earth by His blood shed for us. But Jesus's work to establish innocence is not the same as man's work. Jesus actually *rested* in the midst of His *work* on the cross, simply waiting for His exaltation to glory to come to Him from His Father. He knew He lacked nothing and that the Father's promise to Him was true. And when that work of rest on the cross was complete, God raised Him from the dead, establishing a Sabbath day for us to rest in. Jesus's work of rest on the cross provides us a rest that we can enter into, whereby we can cease from our efforts to establish favor with God, for His work tells us we are the possessors of favor with God. This is where innocence is found. All is well between you and God because Jesus's life testifies to it!

Jesus actually rested on the cross, knowing that He lacked nothing, because He was the Son of God. Even so, we can rest from our labors, knowing we too are the sons and daughters of God. For when the eternal life that is found in Him is fully established in our hearts, there is no need to strive for life. It is this rest that gives us confidence in life, enabling us to live a life free from any external rules or constraints and the manipulation of men, with our hearts and souls and minds restored to a state of innocence. The Bible calls this justification. God is crying out to all men through Jesus on the cross, saying, "I have loved you from the foundation of the world fully apart from your works, and My display of love for you on the cross confirms this reality." As the writer of Hebrews says, so I say to you now, "Do not harden your hearts to this truth as they did in the days of old, thus failing to enter into that rest. But rest!"

Concerning this rest, the writer of Hebrews says this crazy thing, "For all who enter God's rest, rests from his own work, even as He did from His." Now this may be the most bizarre, wonderful thing you have ever heard, but to enter His rest, you have to quit working! You have to quit working for righteousness, quit working for eternal life, or for the acceptance and approval of others. You have to quit working, or there will be no rest! But when you quit; oh how good life becomes! Jesus's one ultimate, eternal command to us is simply this, "Abide in My Love for you." As we abide or rest in His love for us, love overflows to everyone around us, and our lives become natural and innocent. This is what it means to function as Him; it means to simply be who you are, infused with eternal life.

Understanding these things enables us to see how fully complete we are in Him. Here the need for external rules and constraints begins to fall away and be replaced with something far better—love. For in Christ, you are complete. This is the place we find the Spirit of Jesus intertwined with ours and we begin operating from that Spirit. The result of all this is that we find ourselves free from the control and opinions of others. For where this Spirit manifests its life, nothing else has the power to move or control our actions. This provides us the stability and confidence we need to simply live according to the desires of our hearts.

As frightening as this may sound, a life of pure unadulterated freedom is the only way the life of God can manifest itself in human life properly. Either the Spirit of Jesus is controlling us, or something else. As His Spirit of love begins to motivate our actions, we become free to live from the passions of our hearts, which are now fully energized by His life. This is true and firmly established for us, because through the Spirit we have been made partakers of the divine nature and possess everything pertaining to life and godliness.[158] This is the very freedom that God has called you to![159]

Freedom is walking in the infinite love of God fully apart from your work and effort. This is how innocence is re-established in your heart. His indwelling love will show you what is profitable for you in life and what may not be so profitable. His love is the only law you need. For as the scriptures teach, "It is God who works in you to *will* and to *do* His good pleasure."[160] In other words, He develops within us the desire and ability to do the things which are solely instituted by the love of God manifested in our hearts. All the things religion teaches us we need to 'do' or to 'perform' is just that; a performance! It's not real. But

---

[158] 2 Peter 1:3.
[159] Galatians 5:1.
[160] 2 Corinthians 4:12

God is real, and as we begin seeing His love for us more and more, that love produces in us His fruit. Then, every single thing you do becomes His work. So quit acting and just live!

He loved us from the beginning and He loves us now; not because of what we do but because we are His children. We are designed to operate as such. A slave cannot operate as a son, nor does he remain in the home forever.[161] But a son has full access to all the father possesses; provisions for life that are inexhaustible. His love infuses us with these provisions. The scriptures teach us that one day we will be revealed to all creation for who we are. And it is at that point when all creation itself will be released from its captivity of bondage and released into the glorious freedom of the children of God; even unto eternal life![162] His love for us, beheld in our hearts, radiates a glory capable of enlivening the whole of creation. With this in mind I ask you. Do you need anything else?

---

[161] John 8:35
[162] Romans 8:18 – 21

Chapter 12

Conclusions

I hope what I have shared in this book leaves you with a far clearer understanding of the Lord's thoughts and intentions toward you. He is faithful and true toward you and the intent and purpose in His heart never changes. Everything in Him is meant for your good. There is a real simplicity to the truth of Christ, yet somehow religion often departs from that simple truth in the establishment of itself. [163] Listen to these words from the apostle Paul as he was leaving the believers in Ephesus. This was the last time they would ever see him, so his last word were very important to them, and to us.

> Keep watch over yourselves and all the flock of which the Holy Spirit has made you overseers. Be shepherds of the church of God, which he bought with his own blood. I know that after I leave, savage wolves will come in among you and will

---

[163] 2 Corinthians 1:12.

not spare the flock. Even from your own number men will arise and distort the truth in order to draw away disciples after themselves. (Acts 20:28–30)

Apt words I must say. They communicate to us that after the Word of God came to these believers, Paul knew there would be those who would come in to steal the freedom and joy and innocence that were reestablished in their hearts by the hearing of the gospel. Do not let anyone steal joy and innocence from you. You are innocent! Walk in that truth. As you grow in the infinite depths of the simplicity of this truth, and find the power which is derived from it, you will find it is the only form of godly teaching which exists.

Don't let anyone tell you how to live your life, where to go, and what to do! God will direct the steps of your life as you walk in love. There was a man who lived a very long time ago whose name was Enoch. The scriptures do not say a great deal about him, but there is a profound mystery and great meaning revealed to us in the little we are told about him. It says, "Enoch walked with God; and was no more, for God had taken him."[164] In this short exposé we read about Enoch, we see God's whole purpose for our lives, even into eternity. It speaks of us simply walking with God, and as we do, the God of the universe begins manifesting Himself in us. As we walk with Him we begin to think like Him. His thoughts and actions begin to become our thoughts and actions. This is the same way Jesus lived as

---

[164] Genesis 5:24.

He told the people of His day, "The Son can do nothing of himself, but what he seeth the Father do: for what things soever *he* doeth, these also doeth the Son likewise."[165] This life within us and fellowship with the Spirit produces in us great hope and an attitude toward life that refreshes us continually.[166]

I have not addressed everything the scriptures have to say to us in these writings, and that's okay. Not only is it okay, but it's wonderful! For if it is true what the Lord said, "As high as the heavens are above the earth, so are My ways than your ways, and My thoughts than your thoughts,"[167] we all still have much more of the depths of His love to discover. But what I do know I have provided you in the words of this book. I know this to be the foundation upon which all is to be built, for it is true and sure. What I have written is meant to help reveal the heart of God toward all men. This heart is revealed to us in the meaning and purpose of the cross, that is Christ's death, burial, resurrection, and Jesus's ascension to glory. The revelation of all of scriptures, both the Old and New Testaments, has to stem from this foundation, for there is no other foundation than Christ.[168] His heart says to you, in effect, "I love you and have loved you from the beginning, for you have been with me from the beginning."[169]

It is impossible to look at all the differing aspects of the scriptures and fully understand them unless you first come

---

[165] John 5:19 KJV.
[166] John 4:14.
[167] Isaiah 55:9.
[168] 1 Corinthians 3:11.
[169] John 15:27

to grips with the whole of scripture. Because Jesus "is" the Word of God, we find that He is the "whole of scripture." He is the one of whom the whole of scriptures speak! When we look at Jesus's life, his death, and his resurrection unto glory, we can see specifically what His word is speaking to us and about us. We finally come to understand the whole. He alone can make sense of the jots and tittles of the scriptures for us. Just as no one, by studying a thousand individual trees, can truly see or appreciate the glory and majesty of the forest. So, no one, by studying a thousand disjointed verses of scripture, will ever see the glory and majesty of God. The revelation of the glory and majesty of Christ, does not come to the human heart through somehow intellectually piecing things together. It comes to us through the understanding that all the scriptures are meant to reveal Jesus to us. For as the scriptures say, "the testimony of Jesus is the spirit of prophesy."[170]

The great religious leaders of Jesus day sought to understand God through their own intellect, and Jesus addressed this with them. He said (to paraphrase), "You search the scriptures believing that by them you possess eternal life, yet these are the scriptures that testify of me, and you refuse to come to me to have life."[171] These learned religious leaders completely missed the very one of whom the scriptures spoke of, seeking instead to interpret through the filter of *a lie, through their own knowledge of good and evil. Believing godliness and eternal life was attained by the work of our own hands in this fashion, they completely misinterpreted the scrip-*

---

[170] Revelation 19:10
[171] John 5:39.

tures. They stumbled over the stumbling stone, Jesus.[172] Yet those who were wise, the prophets and others, those who simply and honestly desired the truth, pursued something else. They sought after the meaning hidden *behind* the letter of the scriptures. They realized there was more to this story than meets the eye. They realized these scriptures were speaking of a person who would provide them what they could *not attain on their own*, the glory that would follow the suffering of Christ. Their search brought them to what they were seeking. They found the One who could fulfill their lives, give them eternal life and the internal goodness they so desired. Listen to how Peter communicates this.

> Concerning this salvation, the prophets, who spoke of the grace that was to come to you, searched intently and with the greatest care, trying to find out the time and circumstances to which the Spirit of Christ in them was pointing *when he predicted the sufferings of Christ and the glories that would follow*. It was revealed to them that they were not serving themselves but you, when they spoke of the things that have now been told you by those who have preached the gospel to you by the Holy Spirit sent from heaven. Even angels long to look into these things. (1 Peter 1:10–12 NIV, emphasis added)

---

[172] Romans 9:30–33.

Neither God's prophets, nor even the angels in heaven, fully grasped the glory, majesty and power found in Christ. It took Jesus to manifest Himself in the earth for the people to understand this one thing—God is love!. This revelation was meant for us, to whom the fulfillment of the ages has come.[173] Yet even today when scriptures are taught, they are viewed as a book of rules and principles to guide life. This perspective of the Word of God is very weak. Viewing the scriptures this way, men exchange the glory of the immortal God, and our being made one with Him, for a list of rules and principles; believing that by them they can attain a better life on earth. There is no real power for life therein, neither is there any real hope found in viewing God or the scriptures in this way. Honestly, any such thought is ridiculous. But this is what we see in most of Christianity. As we begin to see the truth of the fullness we possess in Him, the Spirit begins revealing to us who we really are to Him. Yes, even the angels long to look into these things. Understanding in these matters is reserved for those who possess a simple desire to know the truth. This desire within us begins to enable the Spirit of Truth to begin shedding light upon the children of truth. This Light manifests faith hope and love in the heart of the believer, enabling us as we develop a Spirit of understanding.

The truth we find revealed in Jesus confirms for us, deep within our hearts, that we are the possessors of an immortal, incorruptible life that cannot be impinged upon, a life in which we can see ourselves as fully forgiven and justified before Him in love. Because we are in Jesus and

---

[173] 1 Corinthians 10:11

He is in us, we possess everything we need for life and godliness. This is the same life that is found in His Son and in all those who see themselves one with Him. Nothing else is required. Yet the carnal mind, in particular the mind grounded in religion, cannot grasp this reality. "Surely we must do something. Surely God requires something of us. Surely human behavior needs some external means of control."

No! All Jesus wants you 'to do' is to see and abide in His love for you. The fruit of that spirit will produce in you the peaceable works of righteousness. And that righteousness is trust in God.[174] As a branch cannot produce fruit unless it abides in the vine, so in Christ we abide in His love for us. The fruit of this life is all the faith, hope and love that are found in Him. As we focus on that love, we find this fruit pouring out to others in our lives. Not because of our love for him, but as a result of our being immersed in the truth of His love for us! Your outward behavior will be as one blown by the winds of love. "No one knows from whence it cometh or whither it goeth." This is the only way to live life, for this life is exciting and good. Because you are in Him and He Himself is blameless, you find yourself blameless—the very definition of innocence!

I leave you with this thought, for it proves everything I have said is true. As Jesus was dying on the cross, there were two men being crucified with Him. The Bible refers to them as *malefactors* one on each side of him. A malefactor is a criminal. Understand that not everyone who committed a crime in Jesus's day was crucified, only the most

---

[174] 1 Peter 1:21.

heinous offenders or those deemed too dangerous to live. So here are these two criminals hanging on each side of innocence. The scriptures say that *both* of these men hurled abuses at him.[175] Then, at some point, something changed, and these words were exchanged there:

> And one of the malefactors which were hanged railed on him, saying, If thou be Christ, save thyself and us. But the other answering rebuked him, saying, Dost not thou fear God, seeing thou art in the same condemnation? And we indeed justly; for we receive the due reward of our deeds: but this man hath done nothing amiss. And he said unto Jesus, Lord, remember me when thou comest into thy kingdom. And Jesus said unto him, Verily I say unto thee, today shalt thou be with me in paradise. (Luke 23:39–43 KJV)

Now the religious, or carnal mind, would interpret these events this way, "So one of these criminals came to his senses, repented of his sins and Jesus forgave him." But the Spirit reveals a much different scenario. What was actually happening here was that a man's heart was deeply affected by the love of God. Even in the midst of having been falsely accused and cruelly treated by His tormentors, this man observed only love and forgiveness pouring out of Jesus toward them all. This love captured the heart of

---

[175] Matthew 27:44.

the man and actually became revelation to Him. It enabled him to see who Jesus actually was, as he tells Jesus, "Lord remember me when you come into your kingdom." This man entered paradise that very day fully apart from his works, good or evil, and regardless of the fact that he was a convicted, heinous criminal. The love of God, as seen in Jesus, elicited within this man's heart a love toward Jesus and the desire to be with Him. This is all Jesus desired of him, and of us!

As human beings, our actions are often far from innocent. But our person, the essence of who we are as people, is seen as innocent by God as depicted in these events seen at the cross. For God was "in Christ," reconciling the world unto Himself.[176] It is as if, through the innocence that was in Jesus, He could see us as innocent as Jesus uttered those words to the father, "forgive them, for they know not what they do." Oh, what love! Jesus saw who we truly were, valued us greatly and died our death for us. He partook in death for all men, that the spirit of innocence which so animated His life, might be in us and animate our lives even unto eternal life. In life there is only one view and opinion of you that matters, God's. When that opinion is right, everything in life becomes right. And in Jesus, This is that testimony!

> We accept man's testimony, *but God's testimony is greater because it is the testimony of God*, which he has given about his Son. Anyone who believes in the Son of God

---

[176] 2 Corinthians 5:19.

has this testimony in his heart. Anyone who does not believe God has made him out to be a liar, because he has not believed the testimony God has given about his Son. And this is the testimony: *God has given us eternal life, and this life is in his Son. He who has the Son has life; he who does not have the Son of God does not have life. I write these things to you who believe in the name of the Son of God so that you may know that you have eternal life.* (1 John 5:9–13, emphasis added)

It is a very good thing to be at peace. The day we see ourselves in Him, is the day we see judgment (as we once understood judgment) is over. The flesh is that which judges. It judges everything and everyone. The Spirit judges not, for in the Spirit we find ourselves one with God, and the need to compare ourselves with anyone is no longer a necessity. As we see ourselves in Him, we find that no offense can come against us that can harm us; we find ourselves totally secure.

It is a very good thing to be enabled to simply be who we are. Pretending and acting is very tiring and wearies the heart; it can now cease. Because we have been made one with Him, just as *He is,* we can simply *be* who we are.[177] There is something marvelous about finding ourselves clothed in Jesus.[178] Those of us who have believed can see

---

[177] 1 John 4:17.
[178] Galatians 3:27.

ourselves wrapped in Him and the glory of God, possessing the eternal, indestructible life that comes from God Himself. We can walk in the full awareness that all is right between us and God, and that His love for us is no different than the love He has for Jesus Himself. God no longer looks upon our sin, ever. Our lives are hidden with God in Christ—swallowed up in life, and one day soon our physical bodies will be also.

God desires all men to experience the free gift of eternal life and the life of peace that comes along with it. Just as the thief on the cross saw the love and acceptance of God in the face of Christ and believed Jesus's testimony toward him, so we too can see that same love and acceptance exists toward us, and believe unto eternal life. All who believe this way find themselves standing in his good company! This is the kind of God I like![179]

The life we have always dreamed of is now ours! This life is filled with all the faith, hope and love that is found in Christ Himself. The truth of how God views us, as seen in Jesus, communicates to us a warm love which permeates the deep recesses of our souls, reestablishing in our hearts the innocence for which we were designed. This is the place where you find a great passion for life manifesting itself naturally, where the things *you do* are not the object of your attention but are simply born from a life that has been set free.

Genuinely happy people are very productive and fruitful in life. People are drawn to such a person. They see in them something they deeply desire for themselves; a joyful

---

[179] 1 Timothy 1:15–17.

exuberance for life and sincere hope for the future. Jesus' love and acceptance for you, His Spirit, brings this to life in you. He is a friend like no other, one who empowers you to love life and people even in the most difficult of times; for He is your Life. No one can impinge upon or affect the indestructible, incorruptible life He has given you. Embrace the innocence and eternal life Jesus has established in your heart through faith in this unshakable love. For this is the sole duty of man.

About the Author

Coming into a relationship with the Lord somewhat later in life proved to be of great benefit to our author Maurice Cabirac. Having spent half of his sixty-six years knowing of Christ in an intellectual fashion, as opposed to an experiential knowledge of the Lord which is attained to through salvation, enables him to see clearly the differences of life 'before' and 'subsequent to' salvation. His years of experience in life has enabled him to see clearly the tremendous effects of what the revelation of the grace of God can do in the human heart. This book is a testimony of what the simple truth of grace, unfettered by tradition, is capable of producing in us.

CPSIA information can be obtained
at www.ICGtesting.com
Printed in the USA
FSHW021803101019

9 781644 588048